Vibrant Life:

1886-1942 Trenton's Italian Americans

To Remo Conti
with the warmest
of wishes

Erasmo Ciccolella

Vibrant Life:

1886-1942 Trenton's Italian Americans

Erasmo S. Ciccolella

1986

Center for Migration Studies of New York, Inc.

The Center for Migration Studies is an educational non-profit institute founded in New York in 1964 to encourage and facilitate the study of sociodemographic, economic, political, historical, legislative and pastoral aspects of human migration and refugee movements. The opinions expressed in this work are those of the author.

This text is a co-publication between the Center for Migration Studies and the National Italian American Foundation.

Vibrant Life:
1886-1942 Trenton's Italian Americans

First Edition

Center for Migration Studies
209 Flagg Place, Staten Island, New York 10304-1148

Library of Congress Cataloging-in-Publication Data

Ciccolella, Erasmo S.
Vibrant Life: 1886-1942 Trenton's Italian Americans

Includes index

1. Italian Americans — New Jersey — Trenton — History

2. Trenton (N.J.) — History. I. Title

F144.T79I83 1986   974.9'6600451   86-6828

ISBN 0-934733-00-7 (Paperback)

Acknowledgments

To the many persons without whose assistance I would not have been able to bring this work to completion go my very warm thanks.

For their unfailing grace in submitting to questions and for being so generous with their time, I must first thank Alfonso Bilancio, Frank Borgia, Vincenzo Campo, Francesco Carmignani, John Conte, Carmelo D'Amico, Salvatore Piazza, and Michael Schifano. To those who rummaged about or delved into collections of photographs for mementos and shared them with me, I extend my thanks: Lena Lo Bue Ballner, Vito J. Brenna, Nicholas Capasso, John Conte, Filomena Sciarrotta D'Amico, Mary Fantauzzo De Bono, Michael Fonde, Dr. Joseph Giangrasso, Hamlet Maisto, Anthony Pacera, Maurice Perilli, Dominic A. Rebecca, Michael Schifano, Antonio Vigliano, and the Trenton Free Public Library. Next I must thank the Rev. James Sauchelli, pastor of St. Joachim's Church, and the Rev. Philip Cordisco, pastor of St. James R.C. Church, for having graciously made available such church records as they could provide. I warmly thank Nicholas S. D'Angelo and Helen Del Monte, members of the St. John's Italian Baptist Church, for allowing me to read the church records. Lena Lo Bue Ballner, Rose Bilancio, Vito Brenna and Leonard Dileo shared their memories of early days with me, and to them I express my deep gratitude.

I am greatly indebted to the following members of city, county, and state institutions which were the major sources of the information gathered: Harold Thompson, Director of the Trenton Free Public Library and Richard Reeves, of the reference department of the Trenton Free Public Library; Editha Starkey, head of the clerical staff at Trenton Central High School; Sandra McDonald and Anthony Fiasco of the Staff of Thomas Mitchell, Secretary to the Trenton Board of Education; Jocelyn Shapiro, of the County Clerk's office; Betty Barker, of the New Jersey State Archives; and Becky Preece, of the New Jersey State Library.

I close by noting that I owe much to wise and patient counselors whose steady encouragement proved to be invaluable: Harry Gerofsky, Robert B. Immordino and Dr. Dennis Starr.

Publication was made possible by grants from the New Jersey Historical Commission and from the National Italian American Foundation.

Foreword

With the passing of time and the passing of men and women who came from Italy to this country in the last years of the nineteenth century and the first quarter of the twentieth century, a haze falls upon those years. The remaining reservoirs of personal and direct knowledge of the life of the immigrants dry up.

It is of some importance, then, that there be kept some account of their rich, vibrant social and cultural lives.

Some Italian Americans born after World War II have rather vague notions as to what their parents and their grandparents did to make life bearable, to make it more than a monotonous round of drudgery. For a few, the still-celebrated feast days of la Madonna SS. di Casandrino may appear to be truly representative of what once was. They are, in fact, no more than a very limited manifestation of what were once mere typically Italian celebrations.

This volume is an attempt at a general overview of events from 1886 to 1942. This span of time was arbitrarily chosen, beginning with the incorporation of the first Italian American organization in Trenton. It begins with a year when there were enough Italians in Trenton to make some collective action possible. It ends with a time when Italian immigrants coming to the United States were virtually completely different from the early immigrants, and when the city and the country to which they immigrated were also much different from what their precursors had found.

Since this writer was brought to Trenton from his native New York City at the age of six, he lived through part of what appears in this account. The pronoun "I" and personal memory, then, have been resorted to from time to time.

It must be noted, too, that the spelling of names has been retained as found in the sources used.

Table of Contents

Whence They Came

I trapiantati, Professor Giuseppe Prezzolini of La Casa Italiana at Columbia University called them − the transplanted ones.

His image is appropriate, for, indeed, immigrants can be compared to vegetative life. Some could barely survive; others uprooted themselves and returned to their native soil − or perished − when conditions proved too unfavorable. But many others found that, though acclimating and adapting were necessary, they could survive in the new soil: the soil was rich if one had the stamina, the determination, and the willingness to work hard and long.

Why transplant themselves to a completely alien soil? For the most part they came because of economic necessity. For others, this land offered the economic opportunity that the political and economic systems into which they had been born could not provide. Others came out of curiosity, for adventure, or for political reasons. Three of these motives are indeed what spurred three members of my family to immigrate to the United States.

My maternal grandfather, Angelo Ruffo, had been a lawyer in Naples. Because he opposed the monarchy and espoused the cause of those who sought to have Italy become a republic, he found it prudent to leave Italy clandestinely, lest he lose his freedom. My father, Salvatore, came here at age 14 with his widowed mother, two sisters, and an infant brother because of financial reverses brought about by a disastrous frost that completely destroyed their citrus orchards. My uncle, Joseph Tallini, migrated twice to the United States. He came the first time, he told me, because "I wanted to see for myself what America was like". He went back to Italy to go into business but, finding that impossible, soon returned here to marry, go into business, and make his permanent home.

In Trenton there live Italian Americans whose roots go back to northern Italy, central Italy, southern Italy, and Sicily. There are relatively only a few from the far north − from the area above Venice and the other northern regions; the greatest number by far are from central and southern Italy, and from Sicily. The regions with the largest numbers of natives in Trenton are Umbria, Lazio, Campania, Puglia, Calabria, Basilicata, Abruzzi, and Sicily. Very few came from large cities such as Rome, Naples, and Palermo; small towns and villages supplied the great numbers that emigrated.

In order that we may know something of the "climate" and the "soil" that these people came from, eight men were interviewed, each representative of a town from which large numbers came to Trenton.

The first of these was Francesco Carmignani, born September 27, 1906, in Trenton, New Jersey, at 41 College Street. As a very young child he was taken to his parents' home town – Monteleone di Spoleto, Province of Perugia, region of Umbria in Central Italy, but he returned to the United States in 1920.

The Monteleone that he left in 1920, he recalls, was a town of some 1500 persons. Most were *contadini, i.e.,* people who worked in the *contado,* the land around the village, town, or city, though their homes were in the town. They could be merely hired hands, working and earning by the day. Others rented or owned land and cultivated it. Much of what was grown by these renters or owners was for family consumption; in times of abundant harvest what the family could not use was sold for additional income. Wheat and potatoes, standard staples, were usually only for family use, while vegetables such as corn, tomatoes, peppers, beans were grown both for family use and for sale.

In Monteleone there also lived those in trades and crafts that served the needs of the people: Mr. Carmignani recalls that there were two shoemakers, four cobblers, two barbers, two tailors, five blacksmiths, four carpenters and cabinet makers, three masons, and two shepherds. There were three teachers (one woman, two men), one druggist, and one doctor.

Though there were five churches, there was but one priest to serve them all. The largest church was that of St. John, but the annual *festa* (saint's feast day celebration) was that of the Madre Misericordia Church, a four-day celebration, from Friday through Monday. The only illumination was by votive lamps in the piazza of the church, and though there were no stands for food or refreshments, the coffee shops, taverns, and restaurants enjoyed a great increase in business during the feast days. The most significant event of the festa was the ascension of a gaily-colored, hot-air balloon.

There were no social or mutual aid organizations, but a number of women were engaged in church-related activities and the men played cards and socialized in the town local, the Osteria di Paolino. Once a year the people went on a Sunday to a sanctuary one mile out of town for the Celebration of the Cross. The one theater in town served usually only as the place where chestnuts and oatmeal were distributed after the blessing of the field animals.

Alfonso Bilancio, born August 2, 1893, in Casandrino, Province of Naples, Region of Campania, was educated at the elementary school and the *ginnasio,* roughly comparable to our junior high school plus some of our high school. He emigrated September 21, 1910 to be reunited with his four brothers, who were living at 252 Elmer Street, Trenton.

He remembers that Casandrino, a town of some 2000 inhabitants, had two churches and a school with five grades. The celebration of the *Festa della Madonna SS. di Casandrino* was held in the first week of September, with street illumination, procession, two bands competing for a prize, and elaborate fireworks. For other feasts, the townspeople went to nearby towns and to Naples.

One pleasant activity was serenading by mandolin. There was no theater, but many would go to the theater in neighboring Grumo Nevano or to Naples. What other activities there were were church-sponsored.

Mr. Bilancio remembers that there were two teachers (a monk and a woman), one lawyer, one druggist, three shoemakers, five tailors, and a number of seamstresses. Some 15 small industrial plants which bleached and prepared hemp employed a small number of men. Almost all the others were contadini.

John Conte, born July 12, 1902, in Grumo Nevano, a town of about 4000 persons, four miles from Naples, remembers that in the town were three doctors; three lawyers; seven teachers — two kindergarten teachers, and one for each grade; and one construction engineer. In the town there were three dyeing plants; looms for weaving sheeting of linen and *canapa* (hemp); and a hosiery factory. There were about 10 tailors; nine seamstresses, 10 bakers; 15 barbers; three umbrella makers; four young men, traveling salesmen of various items or wares, who served outlying towns and villages; one undertaker; three slaughterers and butchers; one maker of fireworks. Virtually all the others were contadini.

Grumo Nevano had eight churches, one being the church of San Tammaro, patron saint of the town. Each of the churches celebrated the feast day of its saint, but the feast day of San Tammaro was the principal celebration because it was for the whole of Grumo Nevano and was enjoyed by all the townspeople. While the minor feasts were limited to one street and one band and fireworks for these feasts were made locally, the feast of San Tammaro was held in the four important streets of Grumo Nevano and boasted of three bands. The fireworks were made by outside talent and featured two midday rockets and a splendid display on the last night of the celebration.

For entertainment there was one cinema. Many went to Naples, readily accessible by trolley car, where they could enjoy motion pictures, plays, museums, saints' feast days such as those of Our Lady of Mount Carmel on July 16 and the feast of San Gennaro on September 19, when the faithful went in great numbers to be present for the miraculous liquefaction of the Saint's blood. One of the most popular festivals was that of Piedigrotta in the first week of September, when the new Neapolitan songs for the coming year are presented to the public at a musical extravaganza. A few enjoyed an evening of opera in the early eighteenth century Teatro San Carlo.

In Grumo Nevano there was limited club life. One found the *Circolo* (Club) *Domenico Cirillo*, named for an illustrious son of the town; two clubs run by and for contadini; and the *Circolo Sportivo*. Social life for the women of the town was to be found in the extended family, among friends and neighbors, and in church-sponsored groups. For the many men who could not join any of the few clubs, there were the Sunday morning gatherings in the piazza and small groups that met for talk and cards in the local *cantine* (wine shops) and *trattorie* (small restaurants).

The town had one dramatic group whose principal activity was the annual presentation of *La Cantata dei Pastori*, the traditional Nativity play. For Lent the people would hang up a female figure of *la Quaresima* (Lent) with nuts and candies dangling from it; this figure would then be shot down on Holy Saturday and the nuts and candies would be distributed among the children. On Easter Monday some of the town's artisans would build a float decorated with floral arrangements. Men would take seats on the float, play mandolins and guitars, and sing. The float would be drawn by oxen to Caserta, where the float would stop for lunch at a trattoria or go on to picnic on the grounds of the famous mid-eighteenth century royal palace. Mr. Conte remembers seeing in Italy a photograph of just such a float that his father Michele, a florist, had decorated for a similar celebration in Trenton.

Frank Borgia, born October 19, 1907 in Melicucca', Province of Reggio Calabria, in the Region of Calabria, emigrated with his mother and sister in February of 1920, settling in Hackensack, New Jersey. He came to Trenton in 1935 to teach Italian and the other Romance languages in Trenton Central High School.

Melicucca', situated on the side of the foothills of Aspromonte, the second highest mountain in southern Italy, was home to some 2000 people in 1920. There were three olive oil plants as well as two flour mills that rendered service to the growers of olives and wheat. In the town there were about eight shoemakers, two cobblers, six tailors, six seamstresses, a few women with looms for the weaving of cloth, a few women who spun thread, eight barbers, one druggist, two doctors, a few lawyers who did not practice their profession, four teachers (two men and two women), two stone masons, one blacksmith, and a few cabinet makers. Almost all the others were contadini, whose vegetables and fruits supplied the daily needs of the townspeople.

There were five churches and the chapel in the house of the local man of wealth. Although each of the churches celebrated its own saint's feast day with street illumination, fireworks, band concerts, and vendors of food, the outstanding feast was that of St. John. The town had its own band, whose bandmaster was also the teacher of music.

There was one social group open only to the elite of the town – the mayor, the priest, and the professional men. For the masses, entertainment was to be had during the saints' feast days, in family gatherings, and in *scampagnate* (picnics, outings). For the women there were church affairs; for the men, talk and card games. There was no theater. Only during celebration of the saints' feast days motion pictures might be shown — at night and outdoors.

Cavaliere Carmelo D'Amico, born June 21, 1894 in Casteltermini, in the Province of Agrigento, in Sicily, emigrated to this country in 1913, but returned to Italy in 1915 to serve in the Italian army during World War I. He came back to the United States in 1920.

Casteltermini was a town of about 10,000 inhabitants. The churches were those of St. Joseph, Our Lady of Mount Carmel, St. Francis, the Matrice, and the Church of the Passion. The feast days celebrated were those of the Annunciation and of San Calogero on the last Sunday in August. These were celebrated in the traditional manner.

Casteltermini had two doctors, one druggist, barbers, shoemakers, cobblers, tailors, and blacksmiths. There was one school to the fifth grade with two women teachers for the girls and two men teachers for the boys. Most of the men worked as *braccianti* (common laborers) in the nearby sulfur mines. A small number were contadini. Some women were seamstresses; others did fine embroidery on linen.

A second native of Casteltermini to be interviewed was Michael Schifano, *Commendatore Cavaliere di San Silvestro* (honorary titles in recognition of good works). Born May 27, 1909, he emigrated to the United States on July 11, 1921. When he came to Trenton, the family settled in the Sicilian enclave in South Trenton.

He recalls that a legitimate theater was built in 1905, but it later became a movie house. After 1921 outdoor movies were shown. The town was proud of its drama group, which presented *La Pastorale* (the Nativity play) at Christmas and *La Passione* (the Passion play) at Easter. Later, actors from Palermo, the capital of Sicily, came to perform in various dramas.

Mr. Schifano added to Mr. D'Amico's list of churches that of Gesu' and Maria and that of La Madonna delle Grazie.

The people of Casteltermini hosted the Church of the Holy Cross from outside of Casteltermini and its celebration of the Feast of the Holy Cross from May 24 to May 30. The celebrants make an exotic and colorful picture because they dress in the style of the Moors and of the medieval knights who fought for the Holy Cross.

Another Sicilian was interviewed — Salvatore Piazza, born in Villalba, in the Province of Caltanissetta, in Sicily, on October 30, 1892. He emigrated to the United States on June 5, 1913.

He remembers Villalba as a community of some 4000 persons, including three doctors, three teachers, one druggist, two barbers, six shoemakers, four cobblers, two carpenters, six masons, and one tailor. A number of men worked in the cement factory, virtually all the others were contadini.

The town had two churches. The annual saints' feast days — of St. Joseph and of the Lord — were celebrated with the usual illumination in the streets, band concerts, processions, and fireworks. There were no theaters; however, travelling companies of actors came from neighboring towns and cities.

Vincenzo Campo, was born January 10, 1897 on Favignana, an island off the northwest coast of Sicily that is the *capoluogo* (chief town or city of a district) of the district which includes the smaller islands of Levanzo and Marettimo. The whole comprised about 5000 inhabitants. The district had two doctors, one of whom was a state public health doctor, and it had the services of a third who was assigned to the prison located there; it also had two lawyers, two druggists and five male teachers in the elementary school (there was also a private middle school). Several surveyors were employed by the community and a few men worked in a plant that made motors. Three families of masons served the town as did carpenters, cabinet makers, wheelwrights, cartwrights, shoemakers, cobblers, barbers, tailors, and seamstresses. Most of the contadini worked for the landowners, though a few were able to rent parcels of land. As one could surmise, there were a good number of fishermen. Others were employed in the salting and packing of sardines. There was another industry – the cutting of *tufo* (tufa stone) into blocks to be used in building.

Social life on Favignana consisted mainly of what the churches provided. Of the three churches – la Matrice, St. Anne, and St. Antonino – the Matrice Church was the only one to celebrate an annual feast day, that of St. Joseph on March 19, with band and procession. Mr. Campo recalls fondly the St. Joseph tables both as individual family rituals and as community cele-brations.

The town could boast of a motion picture house, in which plays would often be performed by bands of travelling actors. There were two clubs in town – one for the upper element, *i.e.* the mayor, the priest, professional men, and the wealthy; the other, *Circolo dei Cacciatori*, the Hunters' Club, open to all, but only a few could afford the club dues.

From what these eight men recall of their hometowns in Italy in the first quarter of this century we can readily see that the communes in central and southern Italy and in Sicily were very much alike.

In sum, the people generally spoke their regional dialects or the standard Italian learned in elementary schools. These towns had schools through the fifth grade. Only one of the men interviewed spoke of having attended the *ginnasio*. Because genteel or abject poverty was found throughout these regions, all too large a number of children were not sent to school but to work, though there were laws for compulsory school attendance. A number of these illiterates came to the United States.

The church played a significant role in the lives of these people not only because of rites and sacraments which are central to family units – baptism, communion, confirmation, marriage, death – but also because of the festivals celebrated and because of the church-sponsored organizations which provided aid and assistance to those in need.

With few exceptions these towns offered their people very little by way of entertainment. Organizations – except for a few for the elite – were not a part of the lives of these people; mutual aid societies were not mentioned, though such societies did exist in Italy.

None of those interviewed spoke of politics or political involvement, though there were elections for the chamber of deputies; men did vote according to their leanings – socialist, liberal, monarchic, or republican.

And now we shall see how these "transplanted ones" took to the soil of their new home.

Map Of Italy

Towns

A. Monteleone di Spoleto
B. Casandrino
C. Grumo Nevano
D. Melicuccá
E. Casteltermini
F. Villalba
G. Favignana

Regions

1. Umbria
2. Lazio
3. Abruzzi
4. Campania
5. Puglia
6. Basilicata
7. Calabria
8. Sicilia

Off to Work They Went

Farm hands and laborers in the south of Italy suffered great privation under the rule of the Bourbon kings; conditions had not greatly improved after the unification of Italy in 1861, and Giuseppe Garibaldi's populist dreams and ideals had not materialized. For the lowly masses of the south, work was a matter of the greatest importance, and in many families even the very youngest had to work if the family was to survive.

Such industries as existed in Italy were to be found mainly in the north of the country. The government paid little attention to the agrarian people of the south and did little or nothing to alleviate their misery. In addition, the people of the south had to bear the indignity of being looked upon by the northerners as creatures of a meaner sort or of another race.

What was left for the people of the south to do? Those who could scrape together enough money took off for a land where their determination and willingness to work at anything that could provide sustenance could be fulfilled.

Those who came to Trenton found a city where there were iron foundries, iron works, rubber factories, potteries, and − most important of all − the opportunity to venture on one's own by supplying services either by following the trade or craft he had come with or to enter a completely new line of work. For example, my grandfather, Angelo Ruffo, had been a lawyer in Naples. When he came to the United States, he knew no English and he knew no American law. Because he thought that as a man with a profession he should learn a trade that had some relation to literacy, he chose to become a compositor − *i.e.*, a typesetter. He learned the trade and joined the typographical union, of which he was very proud for the rest of his days.

My father, Salvatore, who came at 14 years of age, after two years of schooling became an apprentice to a ladies' tailor in Syracuse, New York. He then went to Rochester to further his training, and eventually to New York City, where he worked with the Mengoni Company. When he came to Trenton, he became associated with quality dressmaker Nellie J. Ryder. Soon after, he was asked to teach tailoring and design at the Trenton School of Industrial Arts. A very close and dear friend of ours, Raffaele Volpe, came from a family of jewelers in Naples, but he had not gone into that business or learned a trade before he arrived in the U.S. When he did come to this country, he became a barber. For the Italians who knew little or no English, doctors who emigrated were looked upon as godsends. So it was with Dr. Raffaele Pantaleone, who came of a long line of medical men of Villalba, Sicily.

The various trades, crafts, and professions that many immigrants brought to Trenton, are included in the list below, compiled from my memory and that of friends.

Giuseppe Alfano - butcher
Guglielmo Alvino - master mechanic
John Conte - electrician
Michele Conte - floriculturist
Antonio Cristofaro - monument maker
Cav. Carmelo D'Amico - shoemaker (not cobbler)
Luigi Del Turco - tile maker
Nicholas Faggella - barber
Carmelo Fantauzzo - carpenter
Pasquale Gervasio - baker of bread
Mario Gherardi - architect
Antonio Guidotti - wood carver
Luigi Landolfi - cabinet maker
Pasquale Landolfi - pastry maker

Benedetto Napoliello - musician, bandmaster
Pasquale Panaro - tailor
Raffaele Pantaleone - doctor of medicine
Vincenzo Pecora - decorator, muralist
Armando Perilli - printer
Antonio Puca - plasterer
Antonio Scannella - blacksmith
Salvatore Scardone - maker of fireworks
Erino Sebastiani - mason

The men who came as unskilled *braccianti* (laborers) and *contadini* (farmhands) found opportunities for employment such as their hometowns simply could not provide.

Among the many industrial plants in Trenton, the following were those where a goodly number of Italians found employment:

Acme Rubber Manufacturing Co. - E. State and Johnston
American Cigar Co. - Division and College
American Steel and Wire Co. - Hamilton corner of Canal
Bay Ridge Specialty Co. - 682-692 Stokes
Circle F Industries Co. - 720 Monmouth
De Laval Steam Turbine Co. - Nottingham Way
Efcolite Corp. - Carroll
Essex Rubber Co., Inc. - Beakes corner of May
H.D. Lee Mercantile Co. - 600 E. State
Home Rubber Co. - Woolverton near Cass
L.J. Mott Co. - Hancock and Lalor

Luzerne Rubber Co. - 85 Muirheid
Pennsylvania R.R. Co.
Princeton Worsted Mills, Inc. - 115 Bloomsbury
Reading R.R. Co.
John A. Roebling's Sons Co. - S. Clinton
John A. Roebling's Sons Co. - Buckthorn Plant
Scammell China Co. - Third and Landing
Standard Sanitary Mfg. Co. - Hutchinsons Mills
Star Porcelain Co. - Muirheid near Dewey
Switlik Parachute and Equipment Co. - S. Broad and Dye
Thermoid Rubber Co. - Whitehead Rd.
Thropp and Sons Co. - Lewis near Greenwood
Trenton Brewery - Lamberton and Lalor
Trenton Dept. of Streets
Trenton Malleable Iron Co. - 525 New York
Trenton Potteries Co. - N. Clinton near Ott
Trenton Transportation Co.
Trumbull Electric Mfg. Co. - 150 Enterprise
Whitehead Bros. Rubber Co. - Whitehead Rd.

It can readily be seen that the plants were very close to enclaves inhabited by Italians or were easily accessible from their homes. In the Chambersburg area, for example, could be found the American Cigar Co., American Steel and Wire Co., Circle F Industries, H.D. Lee Mercantile Co., and Switlik Parachute and Equipment Co., Tropp and Sons Co. Others were not so far away as to be inconvenient.

What may prove to be of greater interest is information gathered from the Trenton City Directories which in addition to the alphabetical listing of Trenton residents, also included a listing entitled "Business Directory". In this appeared the names and addresses of persons engaged in the various businesses of the city. Among the hundreds of names listed in the 1885-1886 Directory were found the following:

Barbers: Nicholas Faggella, 20 E. Front St.
Bootmakers: La Fetra and Hull, 47 W. State St.
Masons: Henry Franzoni, 323 Clinton Ave.

The Directory of 1890 carried the following:

Bakers:	John M. Martino, 118 S. Broad St.
Barbers:	Frank De Lorenzo, 616 S. Clinton Ave.
	Frank Lanza, 616 S. Clinton Avenue
	Morelli Bros., 330 N. Clinton Ave.
Boot and Shoemakers:	Anthony Marolda, Elmer and Whittaker
	Vito Vitelli, 561 Lamberton St.

Confectionery:	Angelo Camera, 205 S. Broad St.
	Joseph Episcopo, 339 S. Broad St.
	Pietro Frascella, 167 S. Broad St.

| Music Teachers: | Vito De Lorenzo, 616 S. Clinton Ave. |

The 1895 Directory listed the following:

| Barbers: | Donato Buchicchio, 102 S. Clinton Ave. |
| | John Cerone, 616 S. Clinton Ave. |

| Butchers: | Ottavio Eleuterio, 712 Roebling Ave. |

Cigar Sellers:	Vito De Lorenzo, 428 Ferry St.
	Joseph Graziano, 114 Perry St.
	John Ungaro, 305 N. Warren St.
	John Zuccarello, 26 S. Broad St.

| Cigar Makers: | A. Tuozzolo, 449 Whittaker Ave. |

| Confectionery: | M. Ferro, 317 E. State St. |
| | M. Leoni, 443 Broad St. |

Fruit Dealers:	A. Camera, 205 S. Broad St.
	A. Episcopo, 339 S. Broad St.
	F. Ungaro, 158 N. Willow St.

Grocers:	J. Lotti, 188 Division St.
	F. Medici, 487 Chestnut Ave.
	J. Metinzi, 715 Cass St.

Saloons:	V. De Lorenzo, 428 Perry St.
	D. Leonardo, 610 S. Clinton Ave.
	(This was Leonardo Dileo)
	J. Massari, Cor. Jennie and Genesee

| Ice Cream Parlors: | Parri & Lorenzo, Broad Street park |
| | V. Pasqualine, 1208 S. Broad St. |

| Junk Dealers: | N. Crecca, 219 Ferry St. |
| | J. Nardella, 423 Bridge St. |

Shoemakers:	Frank Di Marco, 710 Roebling Ave.
	Thomas Radice, 227 Cummings Ave.
	Vito Radice, 1118 S. Clinton Ave
	Nicholas Benvento, 638 S. Warren St.
	John Diodato, 318 Bridge St.
	Frank Delgaudio, 402 Elmer St.
	Louis Giuseppe, 612 S. Clinton Ave.

The following table compiled from the Trenton Business Directories, found in the City Directories at five-year intervals, shows the remarkable growth of the Italian American presence in the business sector of Trenton.

TABLE 1
Trenton City Directories

Business Directories	1885 1886	1890	1895	1900	1905	1910	1915	1920	1925	1930	1935
Accountants									1		1
Advertising agents									2	1	1
Advertising novelties											1
Advertising signs											1
Architects									1	1	1
Artists				1					1	1	1
Auto dealers								1	1		
Auto repairs								1		1	
Auto suppliers							1				2
Bakers		1			3	3	4	10	11	10	13
Barbers	1	3	2	2	14	33	54	47	62	92	106
Beauty shops										4	9
Bicycles, supplies							3	2			
Billiard parlors					3		7	5	9	7	12
Blue prints											1
Bootblacks					3	2		3	5	6	
Bootblacks' supplies								1			
Bootmakers, repairs	1	2	7	10	21	31	45	42	53	63	81
Bottlers						1	2	2	1	2	1
Box manufacturers									1		
Brokers, stocks and bonds										1	

TABLE 1 (Continued)
Trenton City Directories

Business Directories	1885 1886	1890	1895	1900	1905	1910	1915	1920	1925	1930	1935
Building and loan										1	2
Butchers			1		2	3	4	8	3	4	11
Candy manufacturers											1
Cafes									20		
Carpenter, builder					1						
Cement block, concrete									3	2	
Chiropodists								1			
Chiropractors											1
Cigar makers			1			1					
Cigar sellers			5		11	16	18	6	9	6	
Clergymen						1	5	3	6	8	8
Clothiers									1	1	
Clothing manufacturers										1	2
Coal and wood									1		
Confectionery		3	2	9	7	14	23	40	88	82	52
Constables											3
Consular agent									1		
Contractors				1	1	9	9	13	24	33	28
Contractors' supplies							1				
Dairy products								1	2		1

TABLE 1 (Continued)
Trenton City Directories

Business Directories	1885 1886	1890	1895	1900	1905	1910	1915	1920	1925	1930	1935
Delicatessens									1		3
Dentists										2	2
Department stores									2	1	2
Dressmakers									1		2
Druggists							1	2	2	2	3
Dry goods							3		11	20	8
Dryers, cleaners									1	3	1
Electrical contractors									2	2	3
Electrical supplies									2		2
Express, local						1		1	2	1	4
Fish and oysters								1	2	4	3
Florists								1	1	1	4
Flour and feed									1		
Fruit and produce			3	2		3	10	13	24	11	18
Furniture dealers											1
Furriers									1		
Garages								3	5	16	17
Grocers			3	1	19	27	50	89	117	135	129
Grocers, wholesale									4		6
Hairdressers									1	2	4
Hardware									4		4

TABLE 1 (continued)
Trenton City Directories

Business Directories	1885 1886	1890	1895	1900	1905	1910	1915	1920	1925	1930	1935
Hat cleaners								2			
Horseshoers										2	3
Ice dealers									1	4	6
Insurance agents								1	14	11	13
Interpreters					1						
Iron railings					1			1			
Jewelers, watchmakers						1	3		5	3	2
Junk dealers			2	1		3				1	
Justices of the Peace									1	3	8
Ladies' tailors						1			2		
Laundries									1	2	2
Lawyers								2	6	9	15
Leather and findings									2	2	3
Lime, cement									1		1
Locksmith											1
Machinist									2	3	1
Marble, granite								1			2
Mason	1										
Meat, wholesale											2
Men's furnishings								1	1	2	1
Merchant tailors								1			

TABLE 1 (Continued)

Trenton City Directories

Business Directories	1885 1886	1890	1895	1900	1905	1910	1915	1920	1925	1930	1935
Midwives							1			1	
Milliners									1		
Mortages, loans									5	1	1
Motorcyles									1	1	1
Moving pictures							2				
Musical instruments											1
Music teachers		1			1				5	4	9
Musicians						1		3			
Newsdealers										1	5
Notaries						2	1	3	14	16	14
Nurses							1		1	4	15
Optometrists											1
Painting, houses				2			3	4	9	9	12
Paperhangers				1			2	1	9	9	12
Photographers										1	1
Physicians						2	3	6	5	10	18
Pianos, phonographs									2		
Piano tuners									1	1	1
Plumbers							2		3	3	9
Printers, publishers						2	1	2	2	3	3
Produce dealers					3		1				

TABLE 1 (Continued)
Trenton City Directories

Business Directories	1885 1886	1890	1895	1900	1905	1910	1915	1920	1925	1930	1935
Radio, supplies										1	1
Real estate agents						2	1	6	23	20	11
Restaurants						1	2	6	19	31	18
Roofers							3				
Rubber dealers						1					
Sewing machines							1				
Shoe dealers							2	4	3	3	3
Sporting goods											1
Steamship ticket agents						3		1	6		1
Tailors						4	8	11	13	10	15
Theaters								1			
Tile contractor											1
Tin workers							1		1	2	3
Transportation											1
Undertakers							1		1	2	4
Variety stores					5	9	3		14	12	9
Vulcanizing									2		
Wines, liquors			3	1	6	16	12				51
Wine and liquor distributors										4	5

What is to be said of the Italian women in the early years of this century? They were the homemakers. Theirs was the never-ending round of cleaning, washing, darning, sewing, cooking, baking, and bearing and rearing children. The husband was the breadwinner, the wife the pivot about whom all aspects of family life revolved. Yet these women in many instances bore additional burdens. Frequently families took in boarders who shared sleeping quarters and were provided with evening meals, and it was the housewife upon whom this additional work fell. Some families opened grocery stores and it was the wife who tended to the store during the day while her husband was employed elsewhere. Some women also took in bundles of clothing from the H.D. Lee Co. and would frequently work late into the night; this was especially prevalent during the Great Depression of the thirties.

We shall now examine the work experiences of two trios of brothers from the same town in southern Italy – San Fele. We shall focus on what these immigrant brothers did to earn a living, and then see what their children did.

We shall first consider the Dileo family. (The spelling of their surname originally was Di Leo.) The family's first venturer to these shores was Angela Rosa Di Leo, who arrived in 1878; then came her brothers Leonardo and Vito. In 1885, at 11 years of age, Pasquale Di Leo joined his brothers. This account of their work experiences here was furnished by Pasquale Dileo's son Leonard.

When the brothers Leonardo and Vito arrived, they immediately found employment in the Roebling's plant on South Clinton Avenue; eventually Vito became foreman of the yard gang. When Pasquale came, he too went into factory work, though at a factory in Morrisville, Pennsylvania. He was, however, quite dissatisfied and, following the advice of a friend who counseled him to strike out on his own even if it should be by becoming a bootblack, he built himself a shoeshine box and began to frequent the area at State and Broad Streets in Trenton; at that time, Trenton's Municipal Building was situated there. Gifted with initiative and the desire to succeed, in a few years he was able to put two bootblack's chairs just inside the entrance to the city hall. With two chairs he needed help and so he hired a man; he had already become an employer and the owner of a thriving business. In a short time, he was known as "The Prince of Bootblacks".

In 1911, the offices of the city administration were moved to the new, imposing, building they now occupy. This meant a new beginning for Mike, as Pasquale was called, but not as a bootblack in new quarters. He gave up that business to assume the duties of managing the Italian Baking and Trading Co., which he had founded in 1904. He employed two men to make and bake the bread and two as drivers who delivered the bread. One of these drivers was his oldest son Dan, who worked as a bread delivery man till his retirement.

By 1895, the three brothers – Leonardo, Vito, and Pasquale – had joined in partnership and opened a saloon at 610 South Clinton Avenue; later, Pasquale left this partnership and opened a saloon of his own at 255 Elmer Street. Both saloons were closed with the advent of Prohibition. A revealing episode shows how Mike – and many others – felt about their adopted land. When the saloons were to close, Tommy Dileo, Mike's third son, though but a boy, suggested that his father turn the saloon into a "speakeasy", a slang term for a place where alcoholic beverages were sold illegally. The father's retort to this suggestion was, "This country was good to me, and I'll obey the law of the land".

Pasquale was still in business with his bakery, but with depression times in the 1930s and the price wars being waged among the Italian bakers of the area, he felt that he could no longer operate his bakery. He decided to close the bakery and retire; his retirement, however, was marked by a number of profitable activities. He became, for example, an agent for the Tattersall Co. Since very many men were unable to have or find employment during the Great Depression, he would advance money for the coal or fuel oil these people needed; he would then make his rounds every week to collect the 25 or 50 cents agreed upon as the weekly installments.

In addition to this, he bacame a realtor, buying and selling houses; he also rented out a number of properties that he had acquired over the years. Finally, he was also a political leader in the ward.

We have seen what Leonardo, Vito, and Pasquale did by way of work. But what of their children? With but two exceptions their daughters were housewives. Listed below are the pursuits of their children.

The children of Leonardo:
  Frank (1892-1971) - bartender
  Daniel (1894-1972) - in State Comptroller's Office
  Pasquale (1896-1972) - in Court of Chancery
  Catherine (1904-   ) - teacher
  Peter (1906-1979) - teacher

The children of Vito:
  Frank (1891-1948) - crane operator at Roebling's
  Daniel (1899-   ) - State House clerk
  Pasquale (1900-1960) - cab driver
  Leonard T. (1904-1974) - State auditor

The children of Pasquale:
  Daniel (1899-1974) - bread delivery man
  Frank (1907-   ) - plasterer; superintendent of maintenance for Trenton Housing Authority
  Thomas (1909-1980) - bricklayer; operated own gas station
  Leonard S. (1911-   ) - teacher; Director of Health and Physical Education

Peter (1914-   ) - clerk in State Treasury Department
Rose (1919-   ) - nurse

The following account was given me by Vito J. (Willie) Brenna.

The Brenna brothers — Joseph, Vito, and Daniel — came from San Fele, as did the Dileos. When they arrived in the United States and were greeted by a great display of fireworks, they quickly learned that it was not their coming that occasioned the fireworks but the celebration of July 4, the day in 1901 when they first stepped on American soil. Joseph was 16 years of age, Vito 15, and Daniel 11. They were of contadino stock, their parents caring for the animals in the fields outside San Fele.

On their arrival in Trenton, the Brenna brothers went directly to the home of their uncle Donato Pierro, who ran a grocery store and performed such banking services as transferring funds to families in Italy; he also ran an agency for the sale of steamship tickets.

Joseph, at age 20, quickly secured employment in the Roebling's plant on South Clinton Avenue, but he stayed at that work only for a short time. He and his brothers, as they grew older, were taken by their uncle into his grocery business. In 1922, Joseph left to open the Home Wet Wash Laundry; Vito stayed in the grocery until 1926, when he closed the grocery and joined his brother in the laundry.

Daniel, who came to this country at 11 years of age, attended the Centennial School and then entered the Rider-Moore and Stewart School of Business. He went directly from his schooling into employment with the Broad Street National Bank of Trenton, eventually becoming manager of the bank's branch at the intersection of Hamilton and South Clinton Avenues. He then became associated with the Michael Commini Company (steamship tickets, real estate, insurance) and later became treasurer of the Roma Building and Loan Association.

We now turn to what the children of the Brenna brothers did.

The children of Joseph:
Anthony (1908-1959) - employed by the Home Wet Wash Laundry
Vito "Willie" (1919-   ) - employed by the Home Wet Wash Laundry; laundry manager for the Federal Government at Fort Dix, NJ

The children of Vito:
Daniel (1908-   ) - funeral director; owner of the Brenna Funeral Home

The children of Daniel:
Joseph (1920-   ) - medical doctor; surgeon
Anthony (1923-   ) - industrial engineer at Fort Dix, NJ

They Established Churches

When Italian immigrants began arriving in Trenton, their spiritual needs had to be satisfied, but because of the language barrier, no churches could fully meet that need. There was in Trenton a Franciscan friar, the Rev. Peter Jachetti, O.M.C. at what is now the Church of Saint Francis, on Front Street; Italians, however, in what was then the borough of Chambersburg, were some distance away from the Church of Saint Francis.

Father Jachetti, recognizing that he could not serve the Italians in his assigned church, gave up his pastorate in order to start a new church in Chambersburg – Our Lady of Lourdes, which was perhaps no more than a chapel. In 1887, construction of a large, stone church was begun on land purchased by Father Jachetti on Chestnut Avenue. This new church, dedicated in 1890, was called the Church of the Immaculate Conception. Father Jachetti, however, was in his new church but a short time; he was transferred to a new pastorate in Albany, NY, leaving the new church with no clergyman who knew the language of the Italians or their special needs, their customs and their attitudes that set them apart from other Catholic groups.

That the majority of Italians are Roman Catholics is a matter of common knowledge; what is less well-known is that some Italians are members of Protestant denominations. In fact, the first purely Italian church established in Trenton was the Immanuel Presbyterian Church located at 444 Whittaker Avenue and organized in 1899 by the Rev. Vincent Serafini, who was ordained in 1898 and became its pastor.

The second to be founded was St. John's Italian Baptist Mission, which held services in a store on Hudson Street from 1900 to 1910. In 1914, ground was purchased at 123-125 Butler Street for building a church; it was dedicted in 1916 and in 1924 was named St. John's Italian Baptist Church. Its pastor was the Rev. Vito Cordo.[1] In 1915 the *Trenton Directory* carried "Italian Evangelical Church, 109 Butler Street"; the Rev. Vito Cordo was listed as the pastor and the agent was Helen Del Monte, of 123 Butler Street. The trustees were Francesco Di Paolo, Joseph Petty, and Zepito Di Quinzio. The church was organized in 1924 and incorporated and recorded June 6, 1946.

Saint Joachim's Church, on Butler Street, was the third to be founded. Papers of incorporation show the following founders: James A. McFaul, Bishop; Aloysius Pozzi, Rector; Peter Jachetti, Vincenzo Lupo, lay trustees. It was incorporated and recorded August 26, 1901.[2] Next came the Mt. Carmel Presbyterian Church organized on September 24, 1918. The Rev. Nunzio Vecere, ordained in 1916, was installed as pastor.

Saint James R.C. Church, on East Paul Avenue, was at first a mission church of Saint Joachim's in 1919. Vincent Fucci was Rector, John C. Zuccarello and Alfonso Gabriele were lay members. It was incorporated and recorded on November 6, 1931.[3]

Next to be incorporated was the *Chiesa Cristiana della Fede Apostolica*, situated at 76 Vine Street. Recorded on August 23, 1934,[4] its trustees were Vitantonio Rizzo, Nicola Amici, Nicholas Rizzo, Emidio Puglia, and Zepito Ruzzi.

Last to be founded was the *Chiesa Apostolica di Cristo*, whose agent was Calogero Sgro, of 215 Morris Avenue. Recorded on March 12, 1936,[5] its trustees were Calogero Sgro, Nicola Amici, Zepito Ruzzi, Francesco Messina and Giovanni Calamanti.

That there were two Italian Catholic churches seems to be a natural response to the spiritual needs of large numbers of people. The Chambersburg area, where most of the early immigrants settled, seemed to be a logical place for a church, and indeed it was there, on Butler Street, that Saint Joachim's was established; the other, Saint James R.C. Church, was erected on East Paul Avenue in an area that served Italians, many of them Sicilians, living in North and East Trenton.

If one accepts the comment made by John S. Merzbacher in his *Trenton's Foreign Colonies* that "among the Italians one finds that the men are as much in their church as the women"[6], one may conclude that this was true of all – or almost all – Italian men. The converse, in fact, was quite the case. Many Italian men affected an anti-clericalism that kept them from regular church attendance and involvement. Though some men worked diligently before and during the saint's feast day celebration, they were either the small number who practiced their religion or some who were active in the secular aspects of a basically religious affair. The anti-clericals were just that: it was the clergy – not the church or religion – that they objected to. They participated in the rites and sacraments of the church – marriage, baptism, communion, confirmation, and the last rites at death – but they did not as a rule attend Mass. Nor were they contributors to the church, though they contributed to the secular organization raising funds for the annual saint's day feast. This poor support of the church could not be attributed to anti-clericalism alone. One may understand this if one knows that in Italy the churches are supported by income from lands bequeathed to them and by an additional small subsidy from the central government; the offerings of the churchgoers, therefore, were always minimal whenever they might attend church. A few years ago I was told by the Rev. Generali, pastor of the Florentine's church in Rome, that any one of our American churches receives more in one Sunday's collections than his church receives in three or four months.

We shall now see how the pastors of Italian churches helped solve their financial problems, and by so doing brought some entertainment and pleasure into the daily lives of their parishioners. We shall also see what acculturation was taking place.

The following data come from church records made available by the pastors of Saint Joachim's and of Saint James R.C. Churches. Those from Saint Joachim's start with an entry for September 8, 1901 and for the most part, are very brief and general; until January 1, 1905, all entries were made in Italian. The records of Saint James are from the Announcements Book of March 1923 to June 1927; there are other entries for July 7, 1935, to February 1938. It is with these records that we can see the broad range of the varied activities that the churches sponsored; activities run by church groups but with a purely social purpose or with no more than a very tenuous relation to the church will appear in another section.

The accounts of Saint Joachim's Church for 1903 show that the church earned $574.73 from fairs and picnics. With this entry we begin to see the acculturation that was already taking place: a fair was purely an American church activity.

We see that in March of 1908, $75 was cleared from the showing of a motion picture; no title, however, was recorded. Another American note was struck in June of 1909, when $59.60 was raised at a Strawberry Festival; two months later, money was raised by holding a "Dance Entertainment".

In February of 1913 the Young Men's League staged the play, *College Chums* earning $52.25 for the church; in the same month the Italian Ladies' Aid Dance netted $50.20. In March of 1913 entertainment of a more elevated kind was provided: $6.10 was raised by the motion picture *Passion* and $200 by the oratorio *Stabat Mater* both apparently chosen as suitable for the Lenten season.

Other typically American church activities proved successful: in May of 1913 a euchre party earned $184.24, a rummage sale $47.64, and a Sodality Dance $53.05. In July of 1913 a play, *Our English Friend* earned $52.30, and in December a children's play raised $32.10.

In 1914, a dance was held entitled *Rising Generation*, in March the Young Men's League produced a play and in May *Old Man's Dilemma* was presented. Entries for 1915 show that the American game of basketball had become an Italian American pastime, $3.00 having been earned from the game. In January a motion picture was shown; in June and July strawberry festivals, and in October a carnival was held.

In May of 1917 $15.50 was realized from a concert held in the parochial school auditorium and in 1918 a May procession was held, earning the church $33.85. Another typically American touch can be found in the entry for May of 1920 — a minstrel show — earning $53 for the church.

August of 1920 saw two street festivals involving participation by the church — those of San Donato and of the Assumption. These activities brought $140 from Masses and processions to the church. In September, there were the annual festival of La Madonna SS. di Casandrino and the festival of San Tammaro, revered by the people of Grumo Nevano, a town near Naples.

In March of 1922, $26 came from the panegyric delivered during the Mass celebrated for the festival of La Madonna SS. di Casandrino. Three motion pictures were shown in the school auditorium: *The Victim*, earning $91.70; *The Eternal Light*, $101.85; and *The Blasphemer*, $61.77. When the film *Transgression* was shown in May, it earned $54.85.

In August, the procession of San Donato preceded the street festival, and in September the feast of the Madonna of Casandrino was held. In December, the school auditorium was rented for the presentation of *La Pastorale*, the Sicilian Nativity play, which will be touched on in another section.

In April of 1925, the motion pictures *The Avenger* and *The Eternal Light* were shown, earning $30 and $87.50 respectively. In June, $50.80 came from Saint Joachim's Dramatic Club and in August the festival of San Rocco was held.

In April of 1926, $134 came from the production of *The Passion Play*; in October, the film *The Life of Saint Francis* earned $47.35. The processions for the festivals of La Madonna di Casandrino and that of San Rocco in September of 1927 earned the church $115. *The Passion Play*, given again in April of 1928, netted $41.25.

In December, the Neapolitan drama group produced *La Cantata dei Pastori*, the Neapolitan Nativity play, which will be discussed briefly in another section; this earned $41.25 for the church.

From 1929 we find that the entertainments the church provided changed in tone; in October of that year, for example, such films as *Where the North Begins, Safety Last* and *Flight of the Graf Zeppelin* were shown.

In March of 1930 a lecture by Fr. Robotti netted $46.17. In December we find that a spaghetti supper cleared $300.95. *Shower of Roses* a movie shown in April of 1931, cleared $21.19, and in September, $625 came from the running of a carnival.

The Christian Mothers' Club held a dance and showed a motion picture, in February of 1933, earning $25.35 for the church. In May a play, *La Tradita* (The Betrayed One), netted $25.25 and in November the Christian Mothers' Card Party raised $104.55 for the church. Another new touch appears in December: the PTA sold chances when members raffled off a turkey raising $53.40 for the church.

The year 1936 saw $321.50 coming from the sale of Easter eggs, $60 from a Christian Mothers' card party, $250.10 from school chances on a turkey and $200 from six weeks of bingo parties. In April of 1938 the Mary Magdalen Play earned $141.75, and a turkey raffle $180.30. During the next year, Easter eggs, a turkey raffle, bingo and a picnic brought $1750 to the church.

We turn now to the Saint James R.C. Church and its activities as recorded in the Announcements Book for 1923 to February 3, 1938.

On May 23, 1923, a big euchre party was planned for August 10. These parties, almost entirely under the direction of non-Italians, were held with great frequency over the years, attesting both to the pleasure they gave the participants and to the sure financial returns derived from them.

On August 17, the Young Italian American Club held a Dance. Plans were made July 29 for a Lawn Festival and on August 18 a Carnival was held.

March 16, 1924, saw a Saint Patrick's Day Eve celebration with dancing, entertainment, and refreshment, reflecting the community's mixture of Irish and Italian persons. On June 9 a Mr. Tynan was the patron of a dance. In the same year, on August 30-31, the festival of Saint Joseph was held, with a procession as a highlight. And in September the celebration of the feast of San Calogero was held, with a procession at 4 p.m.

Beginning August 5th of 1925 a week-long carnival was held and on August 30, there was the festival of Saint Joseph with the usual 4 p.m. procession. The festival of San Calogero, held on September 21, was celebrated with a sermon in Italian and a procession at 4 p.m.

January 24, 1926, saw the birth of a new organization – the Mothers' Club. On February 7 the Knights of Columbus held a Mardi Gras and the first Mothers' Club dance was held on February 15. *The Passion Play* was presented in the school auditorium on March 31 during the Lenten season. The motion picture *Saint Francis of Assisi* was shown April 20. On October 11, the Young Ladies' Sodality held a dance at which a show entitled *The Victim* was presented. A play in Italian *Il Sacrificio di una Madre* (A Mother's Sacrifice) was scheduled as a benefit performance for November 6, and on December 8 a minstrel show was put on in the Parish Hall.

A dance sponsored by the Mothers' Club was held on January 10, 1927, to benefit the school. On January 28 one of a long series of euchre parties was held by the Young Ladies' Sodality. An Amateur Show was given on February 27. The feast of San Calogero was held August 21, and on August 28 that of Saint Joseph. The first annual indoor fair was held on September 11 and a Bazaar was scheduled for September 18.

The following are drawn from entries in the Announcements Book for July 7, 1935, to February 19, 1938. On July 7, 1935, picnic books were to be returned to the church, and on July 28 returns were to be made for the Saint Anne's Society card party. On August 25 the annual feast of San Calagero was celebrated and the indoor carnival was held August 28-29, with dancing and bingo featured. On September 15 a picnic was held at Washington Crossing Park. The feast of Saint Joseph was celebrated with High Mass and the 4 p.m. procession. A spaghetti supper, with free beer, was held on October 3, with admission tickets at 50 cents each. A benefit dance for the church was held on October 23 by the Young Ladies' Sodality and on

November 14 the Mothers' Club ran an old-fashioned dance. Another spaghetti supper was held on December 25, with adult tickets 35 cents and children's tickets 10 cents.

The Mothers' Club held another card party on January 30, 1936. The Holy Name Society presented an amateur night, to benefit the church, on February 21. *Patricia*, a drama in English, was presented by the Young Ladies' Sodality on March 29, and on May 30 a group of actors from Philadelphia staged an Italian drama, *Senza Mamma* (Motherless), in the school auditorium to benefit the school. A showing of the motion picture *Genoveffa* was sponsored by the Mothers' Club on May 12 and July 12 a picnic was held at Sullivan Grove, Washington Crossing Park. The Chianese Dramatic Company of Philadelphia presented a play and a novelty dance was held by the Young Ladies' Sodality on October 11. The Mothers' Club sponsored a card party on October 22, and on December 16 *The Wyoming Whirlwind* was shown.

On February 9, 1937, Granese's Company staged *The Miracle of Saint Rita* and farces in the school auditorium. Several other events were held that year, all for the benefit of the church: an amateur show on May 16; a motion picture, *L'Uomo del Destino* (Man of Destiny), shown on May 18; another picnic, held on June 13 at Washington Crossing Park; a baseball game played at Dunn Field on August 14; and the Granese Company of Philadelphia's presentation of *Chitarra Romana* (Roman Guitar) on October 17. A full-course spaghetti supper was planned for February 13, 1938, and the last entry, that for February 20, indicates that the motion picture *The Life of Saint Anthony of Padua* was shown in the School Hall.

Now we turn to some of the activities of one of the Italian Protestant churches. Records for all are difficult to come by, but good fortune has provided the following information.

As of this writing, the St. John Italian Baptist Church is the only remaining Italian Protestant church in Trenton and it too is facing imminent extinction. Although the church building at 123-125 Butler Street is for sale, members still convene on Sundays for services conducted by interim pastors who come from Trenton's American Baptist churches of Capital Cluster. This will go on until the building is sold.

Two loyal and faithful members of the church who supplied much of the information are Nicholas S. D'Angelo, born in Vestea, Province of Campobasso, Region of Abruzzi, and Helen Del Monte, born in Trenton. Their parents, like virtually all others, converted when they came to Trenton.

Land at 123-125 Butler Street, upon which to build the church, was donated by the Trenton Baptist Mission on April 2, 1914. Money for the construction of the church came from the Trenton Home Mission Society, from the New Jersey Baptist Convention, and from the American Baptist Convention of North America. The Italian Baptists gave of their time, labor, and money.

Members of St. John's church feel grateful to members of the Trenton Baptist City Mission Society, who came to help the church members in many ways. They came, for example, to teach them English, to help them to acquire citizenship, to offer advice, and to assist them with conversion from other religions. Society members also formed sewing classes and taught various arts and crafts.

From Nicholas D'Angelo and Helen Del Monte came record books of the minutes of meetings of the church officers. There were four such books, the earliest of which, beginning in 1913, was entitled "Book of the Secretary of the Evangelical Church of St. John the Baptist, Trenton, NJ". All entries until 1946 — with three brief exceptions — were written in Italian. Among the recorded meetings, those which follow reveal the varied concerns and activities of the church members.

December 31, 1913. Elected to office were: deacons — Giuseppe Petty, Francesco Bonelli; treasurer — Mr. Petty; secretary — Nicola De Luise; usher — Francesco Pugliese.

A social followed the meeting. A brief religious service was held to greet the new year.

January 22, 1915. A special collection raised $1.02, which was given to two young strangers. The group sent $10 to the Home Mission Society.

April 25, 1915. Twenty-five dollars was drawn from the treasury for the City Mission Society.

May 30, 1915. It was decided that a Holy Supper be held on June 6 at 10:30 p.m.

June 25, 1915. At a special meeting the president proposed that an outing be held on July 5; each interested member was to pay 25 cents.

July 6, 1915. Members were appointed to the Supervisory, the Social and the Missionary Committees.

September 17, 1915. A motion was passed that September 20 (the day Italy became free and united) be celebrated.

April 4, 1916. A committee of three was appointed to visit hospitals, a committee of four to see to holding services in the homes of members, and a committee of four to seek new members.

May 2, 1916. The society planned to hold an outing on May 30, with tickets 50 cents for men and 25 cents for women. Brother V. Cordo suggested that a party be held Thanksgiving evening. A party was planned for election night.

December 5, 1916. It was proposed that the church take the initiative to form a band.

December 31, 1916. Deacons elected for the coming year were Mrs. De Luca, Mrs. Rossi, and Mrs. Cardacino. Officers elected were Armando R. Rossi, secretary; Gerardo Izzillo, treasurer; Orazio Previtera, Bruschi Analeto, councilors.

February 4, 1917. Members were urged to volunteer according to their means to a special fund to help the needy and the sick. It was decided to have a party the evening of the 22nd in honor of new members with music and a short play performed by the young members.

May 6, 1917. A trip was planned to the park for May 30 – tickets 50 cents.

August 7, 1917. A party was to be held every first Tuesday of the month, *i.e.* after business meetings.

September 23, 1917. The Rev. V. Cordo was to be the director of the operetta to be staged.

April 7, 1918. A reception was to be held for the newly baptized.

January 31, 1919. The sum of $24 was set aside for the Holy Supper.

May 31, 1919. The sum of $6 was to be used for Memorial Day. Fifty dollars was to go for the supper given by members for Mr. and Mrs. Cordo.

January 1, 1920. A supper was served from 7 to 8 p.m. by the Women's Club. After the supper, Dr. Mangana gave a talk on Abraham Lincoln, illustrated by means of a magic lantern. A young woman invited by Dr. Mangana from Brooklyn sang a number of songs.

January 28, 1920. It was decided to have a social evening and a raffle.

May 11, 1920. It was decided to hold a party for the new pastor, the Rev. M.S. Solimene and for Dr. Mangana, who was leaving as acting pastor.

July 16, 1920. Plans were made for a drama to be staged October 12.

August 10, 1920. A dinner solely for church members was planned for Labor Day.

September 29, 1920. A committee was named to collect money for the victims of an earthquake in Italy.

December 31, 1920. Plans were made for a supper for all church members to be held in the church basement and for a library to be located in the church basement.

May 1, 1921. Miss Herminsky, missionary, was to spend several months among the Italians for Americanization and for religious work. A picnic was planned to be held in the park on May 30.

August 12, 1921. It was suggested that a proposal be made to hold the Italian Baptist Convention in Trenton in 1922. It was decided to hold a "community" evening on Labor Day and to show a motion picture. The film *Quo Vadis* was to be shown Sept. 7-8. Plans were made for the organization of a Boy Scout troop.

April 2, 1923. A special collection was taken up for the children of member Rossetti.

June 3, 1923. A picnic was to be held on May 30 in the park. (These minutes evidently were written after the event.)

October 18, 1924. On this day an elaborate program was held in the church, the highlight of which was the burning of the mortgage by Elmer Eagen, Daniel Cardacino, and Jerry Quallis. (This entry was taken from a printed program and was inserted here for the sake of chronology.)

December 1, 1924. The church was asked for financial aid for the buying of toys for the children of the Sunday School.

December 7, 1924. It was decided to hold the annual meeting on church matters on New Year's Eve so that a social might follow the meeting.

July 6, 1925. The church was to pay for the transportation of the summer school children for an outing in the park.

December 6, 1925. The trustees of the church were to see to the basketball suits for the team.

November 1, 1926. Tickets, priced at 25 cents, would admit to the motion picture showing Thanksgiving night.

December 9, 1926. Offerings were to go to help pay for the expenses of a Christmas tree.

March 22, 1927. Among committees appointed were one on music and one on education.

December 16, 1927. Five dollars was donated to be used to buy pastries for the Christmas party.

January 5, 1928. The Rev. Bolognese suggested that a musical concert be held the evening of April 14 in the Masonic Hall on North Clinton Avenue. Prof. Sacchetti of Atlantic City was to be in charge of the affair.

March 1928. Plans were made for an outdoor service either in the park on Chestnut Avenue or in Cadwalader Park, if permission could be had. Services were to include a sermon in English by the Rev. Anderson and a sermon in Italian by the Rev. Bolognese.

June 13, 1928. The Pastor suggested holding a bazaar in benefit of the church the week of October 14. The Women's Committee included Mrs. Masino, Mrs. Di Quinzio, Mrs. Del Monte, Mrs. Bolognese, and Miss Bartholomew.

February 17, 1929. For the Easter season, ministers were to be brought in to offer sermons. A motion picture projector was to be rented for Sunday evening showings of religious films.

August 3, 1929. Committees for the Bazaar were as follows: sewing and embroidery, baked food and refreshments, candy and amusement, and art goods and toys.

December 15, 1929. A Christmas tree was to be purchased and plans were made for a New Year's Eve Party including a movie and fun and games.

July 19, 1930. Plans were made for a bazaar to be held in the second week of October, the income to go to the church.

December 13, 1931. It was decided to hold a 10 a.m. Christmas service. On New Year's Eve there was to be a party from 8 to 11 p.m., with a religious service from 11 to 12.

August 7, 1932. Hard times are revealed in the minutes for this date. Heretofore, heating of the church came from the burning of coal; now members were considering using firewood.

October 6, 1932. It was decided to continue using coal by using the proceeds from a supper to be held November 17, tickets at 50 cents.

February 12, 1933. Members found that the Depression made it unfeasible for them to convert to the use of fuel oil.

First Thursday of August, 1934. It was decided that a musical concert be held in the auditorium of the Carroll Robbins School.

First Thursday of October, 1934. The Vosa Band and soprano Louise Masino were to perform.

March 3, 1935. It was decided to convert to fuel oil.

April 30, 1936. Plans were made to celebrate the 20th anniversary of the church.

February 9, 1938. It was decided to hold a spaghetti supper the last week of April.

July 13, 1938. Plans were made for a bazaar to be held during the last week of October.

January 10, 1940. The Rev. Bolognese suggested that four Sundays from February 25 to the third Sunday in March be dedicated to music and evangelization, with outside ministers taking part.

May 1, 1940. It was decided to hold a party in honor of the teachers of the Sunday School.

With great warmth and evident deep satisfaction, Helen Del Monte recalls that the Reverends Vito Cordo, Michael Solimene, and Joseph Bolognese had all attended the Colgate Seminary in Rochester, New York, and that it was through their leadership and with their efforts that the church became self-sufficient and began to serve the community. They helped both men and women to acquire citizenship, made certain that the needy were given food, and helped raise funds for charity through parties, outings, and bazaars. Church members, for example, prepared food at home and gave it to the church to be used for the church-run suppers and also solicited contributions of foodstuffs from local shopkeepers to be distributed to the needy. Money realized from the sale of tickets was, therefore, virtually clear profit. It was the food distributed free during the Depression years that earned the church the well-meaning and appreciative epithet of the "hot dog" church. The church members also saw to it that the ill received medical attention.

Among the church-sponsored organizations that Helen Del Monte mentioned was the Sunday School, of which her father Vito was the superintendent. She recalled the baseball and basketball teams fielded by the Baptist Youth Fellowship. She also spoke of the Dorothy Dowell Mission Society; a missionary circle for teen-age girls, the Guild Girls; the three choirs — the Cherubs, the Juniors, and the Adults; and the Daily Vacation Bible School, run by the church during the summer months. Perhaps the most warmly recalled were the mother and daughter banquets.

From the foregoing one would conclude that had it not been for the need of the churches to raise money, there would have been much less in the way of personal involvement and entertainment for the Italian immigrants in the first two decades of this century. Card parties, dances, plays in English and in Italian, amateur shows, minstrel shows, motion pictures, strawberry festivals, fairs, bazaars, and picnics – all served over the years to provide funds for the churches and enjoyable activities for parishioners.

The Organizations They Founded

Alexis de Tocqueville, perhaps the most astute and perspicacious of visitors to this land, wrote in the late 1830s, "In no country of the world has the principle of association been more successfully used or applied to a greater multitude of subjects than in America".[1] When I read this years ago, I mused idly about how this might apply to the Italians who had emigrated here. This curiosity was further piqued when a few years ago, while reading Giuseppe Prezzolini's observations on Italian organizations in this country, I found a different analysis — one having to do mainly with nomenclature, as one might assume from Professor Prezzolini's reputation as a writer. Then came my exposure to the concept of the Italian American experience as I became acquainted with it as a member of the American Italian Historical Association. Now there were three prods moving me to some investigation.

Tocqueville's comment suggested that the organizing of associations was one of surprisingly great numbers and innumerable purposes; Prezzolini's seemed to rest largely on the names given the societies for, as he put it, *conservazione* - conservation.

Does Tocqueville's observation apply to Trenton? The *Trenton City Directory* could help answer this, for in addition to its listing of names and addresses of residents, it lists entries for businesses, organizations, and city statistics. The year 1900 was chosen because by that year there were already nine Italian societies in the city, according to papers of incorporation kept in the County Clerk's Office, in the Mercer County Court House in Trenton.

The 1900 *Trenton Directory* showed that among the "Orders, Societies & c." there were Free and Accepted Masons, 13; Independent Order of Odd Fellows, 19; Knights of Pythias, 6; Improved Order of Red Men, 8; Independent Order of Red Men, 4; Knights of the Golden Eagle, 4; Ladies of the Golden Eagle, 2; Knights of St. John of Malta, 4; American Protestant Association, 2; Junior Order of American Mechanics, 10; Daughters of Liberty, 5; Patriotic Order of Americans, 2; Patriotic Order of Sons of America, 4; Order Shepherds of Bethlehem, 7; Order Star of Bethlehem, 2; The National Union, 4; German Societies, 19; Sons of St. George, 5; Brotherhood of the Union, 8; St. Patrick's Alliance of America, 4; Non-Sectarian, 3; Catholic Societies, 25; Young Men's Christian Association, 2; Grand Army of the Republic, 7; social organizations, 5; cycling and sporting clubs, 6; canoe clubs, 3; Sons of Veterans, 4; Order of United Americans, 5; labor organizations, 31; political organizations (among these the Italian Democratic Club, Peter Lorenzo, Secretary), 11; miscellaneous organizations, 30. This list includes 264 organizations in a city of 73,307 inhabitants.

Few statistics are available as to the number of Italians in Trenton because the New Jersey State Census A.D. 1895, Township of Trenton, according to wards, carried no numbers but instead names by street address; hence, the number arrived at by counting names that were clearly Italian was 697. The *Compendium of Census* 1726-1905, Trenton, N.J., page 25, shows that in 1905 in Trenton there were 2607 Italian-born persons in a city population of 84,180. From 1895 to 1905, this figure grew by some 1,910 persons. By 1915, the Census showed (on page 36 in the above-mentioned *Compendium*) a total of 4,915 Italians in Trenton and the State Census of 1930 showed a total of 7,524 Italians in Trenton.[2]

Following are data included in the records of Saint Joachim's Church. They reveal the growth of the Italian presence in the Chambersburg area from 1902 to 1923.

1902-1903   146 baptisms, 21 marriages, 35 deaths, inhabitants "about 4000"; Sunday school children: 80 boys, 40 girls;

1913   482 baptisms;
1914   495 baptisms;
1915   556 baptisms;
1916   639 baptisms, 133 marriages;
1918   628 baptisms, 64 marriages; school children: 309 boys, 320 girls;
1920   454 baptisms, 115 marriages;
1921   481 baptisms, 108 marriages;
1922   492 baptisms, 91 marriages, school children: 1060;
1923   491 baptisms, 81 marriages, school children: 904.

By November of 1915, 31 organizations were already incorporated in Trenton. Alexis de Tocqueville's observation shows that for these "transplanted ones" the climate in this country was very favorable and the soil very fertile. The number of organizations grew apace.

Because, as Professor Prezzolini said (I translate), "all the associations of Italians in the United States were associations of conservation",[3] the names they gave their societies did, in fact, "conserve", or as I would prefer "preserve". They preserved in their new land their places of origin, their home towns or regions; the memory of the illustrious men Italy has produced; the memory of certain events in the history of Italy and certain place names just as we think of Concord or Lexington. But there is another type of preservation which Prezzolini touches on all too briefly and which I believe to be the primary purpose for organizing in that day — self-preservation. This was manifested time and time again when the name of an organization included the term *mutuo soccorso* or its initial letters M.S., which stand for "mutual aid". The collective need for aid and assistance in time of trouble could best be met collectively. And there was another kind of preservation which they sought — that of their *Italianitá, i.e.*, their Italianness.

The organizations that set the individuals apart sought less to preserve geography than to preserve language or semantics, although the names of the clubs often represented regions. In Italy one may speak of the Neapolitan dialect. We might assume that all who come from Naples or from towns in Campania, of which Naples is the principal city, speak the same dialect, but at one time there were, it is said, 14 dialectal variants in the city of Naples. Pirro Bichelli, in his *Grammatica del Dialetto Napoletano*, mentions the difficulties in a study such as his caused by the various nuances in meanings and the various pronunciations which then result in varied usage and spelling.[4] Professor Bichelli speaks of today's two Neapolitan dialects – that of the inner city and that of the contiguous or bordering areas. It should come as no surprise, then, that we find clubs representing the regions of Umbria, Lazio, Campania, Abruzzi, Basilicata, Puglia, Calabria, and Sicily. The Italianitá the immigrants sought to preserve might more properly be found in a far narrower sense – their strong ties not so much to Italy, but to their *paese*, which in Italian may mean country, city, town, or village but generally means town. So we find a society named for Caserta rather than Campania, for Monteleone rather than Umbria, for Bisignano rather than Calabria.

Not only do we learn of the geographic origins of the Italian immigrants, but we learn of their devotion to the patron saints of their home towns or especially venerated saints or madonnas. In Trenton even non-Italians may be familiar with the *Madonna Santissima di Casandrino* because of the well-publicized annual feast held in early September. Among other saints revered and memorialized by Trenton societies are Saints Cosma and Damiano (Calabria), Saint Michael the Archangel (Caserta), San Francesco (Bisignano), and San Tammaro (Grumo Nevano).

It has been mentioned that all of the regions from Umbria to Sicily are represented among the Italian Americans of Trenton. Their societies tell us that a good number came from particular towns. Place names in the titles show the following: Bisignano, Cannara, Casandrino, Caserta, Casteltermini, Favignana, Ferentillo, Leonessa, Monteleone, Monterviso, Napoli, Roma, Ruvo del Monte, San Fele, and Villalba.

The Italians also memorialized some of the great figures of Italy, men and women who had made a mark in the arts, in the sciences, in war, and in government. The names that appear very frequently are those of Cristoforo Colombo, Vittorio Emanuele II, and Giuseppe Garibaldi. Nothing need be said of these; their deeds are known by all. The names of others will be touched on briefly to show what the immigrants found to be admirable and significant. Giovanni Bovio (1841-1903) was a political philosopher and renowned professor of law at the University of Naples who wrote a number of essays and books on Italian jurisprudence which were highly regarded.[5] Pietro Badoglio was an Italian general and marshal, Marquis of Sabotino.

Born in 1871, he was widely acclaimed in World War I for his ability to inspire his soldiers and raise their morale, especially in the dark days of the Austrian campaign.[6] Felice Cavallotti (1842-1898) was a writer and a political figure who supported Garibaldi's Sicilian venture. Lawyer and poet, he wrote a drama in poetry entitled *I Pezzenti* (The Beggars). He fought a number of duels, in one of which he fell mortally wounded.[7] Adelaide Cairoli was a woman highly regarded for having espoused universal suffrage[8] and for being a republican.[9] Gabriele D'Annunzio (1863-1938) was noted as a child poet who was eagerly received by the Romans when he left his native Pescara. Internationally known as a writer, he captured the imagination of the masses by his aerial exploits during World War I, *e.g.*, a flight over Trento and Trieste. He was lionized in the U.S.[10] Another to be noted is Cesare Battista, born in Trento, which at the time of his birth was in Austrian territory. A deputy from that city, he maintained even before World War I that Trento was Italian. In 1915 he joined the Alpini, a select corps of specialists in mountain warfare, to fight in the Italian Army against Austria. He was wounded and taken prisoner. The Austrians declared him a traitor because he had been born in Austrian territory and condemned him to die by hanging.[11] Camillo Benso Conte di Cavour (1810-1861) was an Italian statesman and premier of Sardinia. The three – Garibaldi, Mazzini, and Cavour – are looked upon as those who were largely responsible for the unification of Italy.[12]

Names of great figures in the arts and sciences are also found. We find, for example, the Dante Lyceum. We find also the incomparable tenor from Naples, Enrico Caruso. There is also Pietro Mascagni, the operatic composer. In the sciences we find Galileo Galilei. Among the inventors we find Guglielmo Marconi, inventor of the radio. We also find one, Antonio Meucci, who the Italians strongly contend is the real – the true – inventor of the telephone. He lived on Staten Island in poverty, making candles. In a dark period, his wife sold all his materials, leaving nothing to show for his work except that today one may get detailed information from the U.S. Patent Office regarding the patents he sought.

Places also played a part in the naming of organizations. First are the names of importance in recent Italian history. Then comes Trenton – and its distinct areas and its streets.

We have seen that Cesare Battista gave his life for the redeeming of Trento and that D'Annunzio flew over the cities of Trento and Trieste during World War I. Those place names were given to a society in 1920. Another name appears: Tripoli. Italy's successful venture into North Africa in 1911[13] was memorialized when the Tripoli Social Club of Trenton, N.J. was incorporated in 1916. As Prezzolini saw, and as any one can readily see from the list that follows, the names of towns where organizations were founded appear in the names of a number of the societies.[14] We not only find the phrases *di Trenton*, or "of Trenton", appended to the societies' names but we find the names of the sections of the city where the clubs were founded. For example, we find North Trenton, South Trenton, Chambersburg, and the names of streets – Bayard, Butler, Chestnut, and others.

At the very beginning and for years afterward, however, the basic reason for organizing was not to memorialize a town, saint, or historical figure; the reason for organizing was for mutual aid. The first society, founded in 1886, was called a Benevolent Society; the second, founded in 1889, was termed Mutual Relief or Beneficence. Until 1930 virtually all the associations were organized for mutual aid. We may read such laudable purposes as educational, moral, patriotic, and intellectual, but invariably the terms mutual aid and death benefit will be found.

The number of societies formed for mutual aid in Trenton is astoundingly large, especially when one considers that the early immigrants came here with virutally no experience in mutual aid groups. Yet we know that these societies did in fact exist in Italy, because laws had been enacted in 1885 defining and determining what would qualify as mutual aid societies.[15] Only one person of the eight interviewed, John Conte, mentioned that such aid as was available came from three of the churches of Grumo Nevano. Mr. Conte also mentioned other associations and graciously made available a history of Grumo Nevano, from which book the following was taken. Immediately after World War I, a group of war veterans founded a local veterans organization.[16] In 1920 a number of young men created The Costante Girardengo Sporting Club.[17] In the spring of 1921 the Roberto Bracco Dramatic Club was organized; a select company of students, professional people, and artisans – all lovers of the theater – met Sundays for 10 years and staged comedies and serious dramas. In 1935 the company disbanded because competition from talking pictures proved to be too strong.[18]

As has been mentioned, all the men interviewed said that the churches might help the needy in some small way. In Grumo, however, there were four organizations for public welfare: the fund for marriages of Santa Maria della Purita', the orphanage of San Gabriele Arcangelo, the Parolisi-Cristiano Fund, and the Municipal Bureau for Public Assistance.[19] The fund for marriages, harking back to the 18th century, provided poor but worthy girls 25 ducats for their dowry, without which dowry no girl could hope to marry. John Conte's mother, who was an orphan, was the recipient of the dowry. By 1932 the dowry was set at 25,000 lire. The orphanage goes back to the early 18th century, the charges being orphaned girls. The Monte Parolisi-Cristiano, named after the families founding and funding it, provided financial and medical aid for the needy. Oddly enough, there was the national law of August 3, 1863, which stipulated that every commune have an ECA – *Ente Comunale di Assistenza* (Communal Assistance Group). According to

Rasulo, author of the history, in 1927 it grew from the Charity Group, but it did nothing to alleviate the problems of the needy. It was not till 1945 that it was reorganized and proved to be an effectively functioning organization.[20]

Among the early organizations may be found a number of which had to do with labor in general or with trades in particular. In 1903, for example, the *Societa' Operaia Mutuo Soccorso Villalbo* was founded. An *operaio* is a worker. In 1909 there came the Italian Circle of Labor; in 1919 the *Loggia Operaia Savoia*, part of the Sons of Italy, came into being; in 1921 there was the *Societa' Operaia di Mutuo Soccorso Favignana*; in 1926 the *Circolo Muratori Italiani* (The Italian Masons Club) was started; and in 1927 we find the Italian-American Workmen's Club.

Something must be said about women in organizations. In the early 1900s women were active in church societies and in such groups as were created by the Young Women's Christian Association through its International Institute, located at the corner of South Clinton Avenue and Beatty Street. It was not till 1924 that an Italian women's auxiliary was incorporated, the *Societá Femminile Villalba di M.S. di Trenton, N.J.* In 1927 the *Sorelle Monteleonesi di M.S. di Trenton, N.J.*, was founded. In 1928 came the Ferentilese Women's Mutual Aid Socity. In 1936 the Roman Women's Mutual Aid Society was born.

When we get to the 1930s we find many organizations to be purely social, musical, dramatic, or cultural. From this time on we begin to see such names as Bay Ridge Club, Italian Welfare Association, Ferry Athletic Association, Mott Social Club, and Rosemont Social Club. We find, too, that, though the mutual aid societies continued to flourish, many of the clubs were now expressing their purposes to be athletic, social, civic, political, fraternal, and promotive of good fellowship and social welfare.

For people coming to this country with little or no experience in associations, the variety and astonishingly large number of associations founded by Italian immigrants proves the validity of Tocqueville's observation made some 50 years earlier.

The lists of organizations which follow are labeled according to the sources in which they were found.

From books containing papers of incorporation in the County Clerk's Office in the Mercer County Court House.

1   Italian-American Christopher Columbus Benevolent Society (in the Borough of Chambersburg)
    John B. Pirola, president; Francesco Di Marco, secretary; Vito Radice, treasurer
    Recorded September 9, 1886

2   Society Washington and Victor Emanuel Italo Americano or Mutual Relief and Beneficence of Trenton, N.J.

Officers: Angelo Camera, president; Archy B. Prospera, vice president; Alphonso Episcopo, secretary; Giuseppe Di Luigi, assistant secretary; Pietro Jacchetti, treasurer; Antonio Rosati, inspector
Councillors: Pasquale Votta, Silvio Gervasone, Giuseppe Gagliardi, Carlo Sisto, Antonio Mazzoni, Raffaele Ollivetti, Francesco Branca, Carmine Tremetiere, Aurelio Jacchetti, Enrico Bonelli, Michele Lettieri, Cruciano Jacchetti
Recorded January 25, 1889

3 Italian Republican Club of Trenton, N.J., organized Dec. 13, 1892
Vito Di Leo, president; Viti Vitelli, vice president; Gerardo Radice, secretary; Vito Radice, vice secretary; Joseph Massari, treasurer
Recorded December 23, 1893

4 The Neapolitan Republican League, organized March 4, 1895
Officers: Frank S. Lanza, president; Donato Radice, secretary; Antonio Colucci, treasurer
Trustees: Gerardo Radice, Antonio De Lucia, Giuseppe Russo, Vito De Lorenzo, Frank S. Lanza
Recorded February 17, 1896

5 Roman Beneficial Society, organized August 22, 1896
Officers: Peter Jachetti, president; Frank Di Marco, secretary; Bernard Lotti, treasurer
Recorded August 31, 1896

6 The Italian Democratic Club of Trenton, N.J.
Purposes: social, recreative, and literary advancement of its members and for the promotion of the principles of the Democratic Party
Business address: 401 Lamberton Street
Trustees: John Zuccarello, Antonio Ross, Pasquale Lorenzo, Antonio Mark Frascella, Peter Pulone
Recorded February 23, 1899

7 The Joseph Garibaldi Association of Trenton, N.J.
Purposes: educational, beneficial, and patriotic. Provide for the relief of disabled or destitute members or their families; pay death benefits
Business address: 703 South Broad Street
Trustees: Vito Di Leo, Bonifacio Musano, Antonio Mazzoni, Francesco Sisti, Francesco Miele, Angelo Maria Tuozzolo, Salvatore Mulé, Rev. Vincenzo Serafini, Vito Di Lorenzo, Giovanni Zuccarello
Recorded March 15, 1899

8 The Italian Military Beneficial Society (Second Regiment Bersaglieri of Novara), a society of less than 10 members
Purposes: for mutual aid and benefit of members and their families
Trustees: Gerardo Radice, Vito Massaro, Luigi Rotunno, Giuseppe

Carnevalo
Recorded June 20, 1899

9 Same as above
Business address: 622 South Clinton Avenue
Trustees: Antonio Frasanello, Donate Antonio Buchicchio, Antonio Colucci, Michele Ferraro, Pietro Felici
Recorded November 14, 1899

10 Conte Camillo Benso di Cavour Society of Trenton, N.J.
Purposes: mutual aid and decent burial
Business address: 551 South Clinton Avenue
Trustees: Vincenzo Lupo, Vito Dileo, Pasquale Lorenzo, Giuseppe Petrino, Giovanni Pinto
Recorded May 7, 1901

11 *Sossito Colobresse S. Cosimo Edamiano* (non-sense as recorded; should read Societá Calabrese S.S. Cosma e Damiano)
Purposes: relief, mutual aid, and decent burial
Business address: 551 South Clinton Avenue
Trustees: Vincenzo Viteritto, Massimino Asterino, Pietro Felice, Giuseppe Boscarello, Francesco Viteritto
Recorded July 16, 1901

12 The Young Italian Progressive and Social Club of Trenton, N.J.
Purposes: to cultivate social and intellectual relations among its members, and for recreation
Trustees: Antonio Pinto, Rosato Salamandra, Antonio Vitello, John Wilno, Sebastian Faggella
Recorded February 6, 1902

13 *Societá Villalbesa*
Purposes: mutual aid and death benefit
Business address: 551 South Clinton Avenue
Trustees: Salvatore Vizzini, Salvatore Mule', Vincenzo Lupo, Serafino Zoda, Rosario Lupo
Recorded August 30, 1902

14 *Unione e Fratellanza Sanfelese*, Sanfelese Brotherhood Union of Mutual Benefit
Purposes: mutual aid and death benefit
Business address: 314 Hudson Street
Trustees: Vito Massary, Antonio Colucci, Donato Lorenzo, Sebastiano Tonzoni
Recorded September 12, 1902

15 Italian Republican Federation of Mercer County
    Purposes: to cultivate social, political, and intellectual relations among
    members, and for recreative purposes
    Trustees: L.M. Buddo, M.D.; Vito Dileo, Bonifacio Musano, Giuseppe
    Frascello, Frank Radice
    Recorded October 20, 1902

16 *Circolo Progressive Ruvese di Mutuo Soccorso*
    Purposes: mutual aid and death benefit
    Business address: 61 Butler Street
    Trustees: Bonifacio Musano, Giovanni Muccioli, Giovanni Musano,
    Giuseppe Massaro, Antonio Luciano
    Recorded February 9, 1903

17 *Societá Operaia Mutuo Soccorso Villalbo*
    Business address: 503 North Clinton Avenue
    Trustees: Salvatore Vizzini, Michael Zoda, Alfonzo Raimona, Angelo
    Favata, Calogero Riggi
    Recorded February 16, 1903

18 Neapolitan Mutual Benefit Society of Trenton, N.J.
    Purposes: mutual aid and death benefit
    Business address: 18 Mott Street
    Trustees: Fillippo d'Angelo, Rafael Quisito, Frank Banello, John Da
    Bronzo, Augustino Aversano
    Recorded December 21, 1905

19 Neapolitan Juvenile Dramatic Circle
    Purposes: educational; to elevate the faculties of intellectual power, to
    give theatrical performances
    Business address: 589 South Clinton Avenue
    Trustees: Domenico Russo, Giovanni Russo, Giuseppe Maisto, Giuseppe
    Pica, Antonio Di Giuseppe
    Recorded March 12, 1907

20 The Mascagni Italian Band
    Purposes: social, intellectual, and recreative
    Business address: 485 Chestnut Avenue
    Trustees: Joseph Massaro, Vito Alvino, Erasmo Baldaccini, Eugene
    Laugier, John Russo
    Recorded July 15, 1907

21 *Societá Casertana di M.S. San Michele Arcangelo* of Trenton, N.J.
    Purposes: mutual aid and death benefit
    Business address: 714 South Clinton Avenue

Trustees: Gennaro Cardelia, president; Vincenzo Pisacane, vice president; Antonio Gliotto, secretary; Antimo Zazza, vice secretary; Arcangelo Pacini, treasurer
Recorded September 12, 1907

22 Monteleonese Society of Trenton, N.J.
Purposes: mutual aid and death benefit
Business address: 714 South Clinton Avenue
Trustees: Giorgio Calisti, president; Angelo Pierleonardi, vice president; Luigi Di Marco, secretary; Luigi Medici, treasurer
Recorded October 11, 1907

23 The Italian Circle of Labor
Purposes: pleasure, sociability, promotion of the welfare of the Italian people
Business agent: Francesco Mondi, 485 Chestnut Avenue
Trustees: Roberto Misticoni, president; Giovanni Palmeris, secretary; Nello Riccardi, treasurer; Alessandro Fiore, Andrea Francucci, Francesco Mondi
Recorded November 8, 1909

24 The Christopher Columbus Italian Political Club
Purposes: social, educational, political
Trustees: Leo Salamandra, Louis Salamandra, August Vannozzi, Melindo Persi, Daniel Bendivoglio
Recorded October 11, 1910

25 St. Donato Society of Trenton, N.J. of Mutual Aid and Relief
Purposes: to improve the religious, political, and social conditions, and the mutual benefit of its members
Business agent: Raffaele De Luca, 400 Lamberton Street
Trustees: Lodovico Recine, Leopoldo Manzi, Massimiliano Astorino, Antonio Mengoni, Domenico Lapo
Recorded April 15, 1911

26 The Christopher Columbus Memorial Association of Trenton
Purposes: funds for the erection of a monument to the memory of Christopher Columbus; social and recreative
Business agent: Victor Tally, 693 South Clinton Avenue
Trustees: Anthony Roda, Biace Lofredo, Gennaro Giudotti, Sebastiano F. Fasanella, Andrew Koltko, Giuseppe Graminatico
Recorded October 13, 1911

27 Italian-American Independent League
Purposes: social, political, intellectual, and recreative
Business agent: Francis M.A. Rebecca, 137 E. State Street
Trustees: Michael Commini, Anthony Pittaro, Pasquale Antonio Cella,

Antonio Vitelli, Francis M.A. Rebecca
Recorded May 12, 1913

28   *Societá Monterivosana di M.S.* of Trenton, N.J.
Purposes: educational, social, recreative
Business agent: Peter Orsi, 485 Chestnut Avenue
Trustees: Melindo Persi, Philip Corsi, Peter Orsi
Recorded July 8, 1913

29   Favignana Beneficial Society
Purposes: mutual aid and death benefit
Business agent: Biagio Mulé, 127 Mott Street
Trustees: Placido Mulé, Salvatore Mulé, Sarino Agricola, Amilcare
Costantini, Biagio Mulé, Angelo Mulé, Michele Campo
Recorded September 25, 1913

30   *Societá di Mutuo Soccorso Casteltermini*
Purposes: mutual aid and death benefit
Trustees: Salvatore Guagliardo, Vincenzo Giuliano, Benedetto D'Amico,
Giovanni Scozzari, Agostino Butticé
Recorded October 2, 1915

31   *Societá Cattolica San Tammaro* of Trenton, N.J.
Purposes: mutual aid and death benefit
Trustees: Domenico Cristofaro, Raffaele Pezzella, Pasquale Chiacchio,
Gaetano Chiacchio, Giovanni Bencivenga
Recorded November 1, 1915

32   Italian Independent Club of Trenton, N.J.
Purposes: social, moral, and intellectual
Trustees: Antonio Ulla, Angelo Giordano, Carmelo Battaglia, Domenico
Sestito, Fortuanto Sussa
Recorded June 12, 1916

33   Tripoli Social Club of Trenton, N.J.
Purposes: general sociability; entertainment tending to improve moral,
intellectual, and physical condition of its members
Witnesses: Salvatore Colagirone, Salvatore Scamello, Salvatore
Palmieri, Giuseppe Dipranco, Giuselli Midulla
Recorded August 4, 1916

34   Dante Lyceum of Trenton, N.J.
Purposes: educational, intellectual, social
Trustees: Angelo Salerno, Emilio Petrecca, Antonio Di Cesare, Antonio
Di Spirito, Giuseppe Marrazzo
Recorded January 26, 1917

35   Garibaldi Lodge, No. 102, I.O.O.F.

Purposes: aid to the disabled, sick, or destitute; death benefit
Business agent: the Rev. Vincent Serafini, 420 Hudson Street
Trustees: Pasquale Dileo, Anthony Vitelli, Pasquale Maggi, Sebastian Petrino, D.A. Brenna
Recorded January 26, 1917

36   Dramatic Club "City of Naples" of Trenton, N.J.
Purposes: promotion of drama, literature, and art; social and fraternal spirit among its members
Trustees: Giuseppe Maisto, Saverio Conte, Alexander De Rosa, Giovanni Russo, Domenick Russo
Recorded February 28, 1917

37   Leonessana Abruzzese Society of Mutual Aid of Trenton, N.J.
Purposes: mutual aid, sick and death benefit; aid to orphans; general charity
Trustees: Amedeo Rofi, Nazzareno Brandi, Angelo Coiante, Dr. Joseph A. Tempesto, Ciro Cioante
Recorded March 14, 1917

38   Guglielmo Marconi Social Club of Trenton, N.J.
Purposes: promotion of social and educational interest
Agent: Giuseppe Longo, 64 Butler Street
Trustees: Raffaele Quisito, Giuseppe Salvatore, Alfonso Bilancio, Emilio De Colo, Michele Di Pietro
Recorded May 12, 1917

39   Cesare Battista Social Club of Trenton, N.J.
Purposes: improvement of the social, educational, and political standing of its members
Agent: Nicolo Popolo, 270 Elmer Street
Trustees: Pasquale Popolo, Giuseppe Innamorato, Matteo Perrone, Raffaele Quisito, Pasquale Pezzicoli
Recorded May 14, 1918

40   *Loggia "Washington" e V.E. II*, O.F.D.I.
Purposes: mutual aid and death benefit
Agent: Pasquale Dileo, 255 Elmer Street
Trustees: Vito Dileo, Pasquale Dileo, Antonio Mengoni, Antonio Acolia, Giuseppe Di Luigi
Recorded May 21, 1918

41   *Circolo Italiano* (Italian Club) of Trenton, N.J.
Purposes: educational, patriotic; promotion of social welfare of its members
Agent: Enrico V. Pescia, 143 East State Street
Trustees: Dionigi Della Porta, Leo Salamandra, Luigi Salamandra, Luigi

Pianarosa, Michele Commini, Frank Russo
Recorded November 19, 1918

42   Meucci Lodge No. 282 O.F.D.I. in America of Trenton, N.J.
     Purposes: mutual aid, death benefit
     Agent: John Cerone, 271 Hamilton Avenue
     Trustees: Raffaele Giordano, Vincenzo Brangini, Angelo Salerno,
     Fabiano Polombi, Luigi Baldassari
     Recorded December 6, 1918

43   *Societá San Francesco di Bisignano* of Trenton, N.J.
     Purposes: educational, beneficial, patriotic
     Agent: Bruno Varchetto, 414 Hudson Street
     Trustees: Domenico Misciascio, Michele Ammirato, Frank Rago,
     Antonio Arena, Luigi Esposito
     Recorded January 29, 1919

44   *Circolo Calabro* of Trenton, N.J.
     Purposes: educational, patriotic; promotion of social welfare of its
     members
     Agent: Domenico Misciascio, 204 Emory Avenue
     Trustees: Luigi Esposito, Giuseppe Rago, Ammirato Rosalbino, Frank
     Rago, Michele Ammirato
     Recorded January 29, 1919

45   American Falisca Society of Trenton, N.J.
     Purposes: mutual aid, death benefit
     Agent: Giovanni Manganelli, 800 Roebling Avenue
     Trustees: Giovanni Manganelli, Annibale Mazzetti, Francesco Carelli,
     Livio Maurizi, Riccardo Castellani
     Recorded March 10, 1919

46   Italo-American Welfare Club of Trenton, N.J.
     Purposes: moral, social, intellectual
     Agent: F. Martucci, 714 South Clinton Avenue
     Trustees: Pasquale Capone, Giovanni Tomasulo, Daniel Buchicchio,
     Michael Rita, Antonio Grosso
     Recorded April 16, 1919

47   *Loggia Operaia Savoia* Branch No. 688, Order Sons of Italy in America
     Purposes: promotion of social, economical, and political welfare of its
     members; mutual aid and death benefit
     Agent: Angelo Ruffo, 522-524 South Clinton Avenue
     Trustees: Giuseppe Santosuosso, Cesare Ronca, Giuseppe Sacchitelli,
     Biagio Mulé, Pasquale Ricci
     Recorded June 16, 1919

48   Saint Joachim Society
Purposes: to promote, foster and encourage, spread and disseminate
the principles and teachings of the Roman Catholic Church by meetings,
lectures, sermons, literature and all other means consistent with the
objects of this association
Agent: Domenico Buchicchio, 548 South Clinton Avenue
Trustees: Domenico Buchicchio, Raffaele Gervasio, Antonio Vella,
Antonio Bella, Felice Nardi
Recorded June 23, 1919

49   Antonio Meucci Team Club
Purposes: advancement of education among members, interest in civic
affairs, promotion of fraternal spirit among members
Agent: Michael Commini, 307 Hudson Street
Witnesses: Michael Commini, Frank Russo, Gaetano Di Donato, Michele
Carlucci, Mauro Frascella, Thomas Commini, John Cerone, Nicholas
Del Gaudio
Recorded December 29, 1919

50   *Societá Trento e Trieste di Trenton, N.J.*
Purposes: mutual aid and death benefit
Agent: Giuseppe Croce, P.O. 66, Trenton Junction, N.J.
Trustees: Giuseppe Croce, Giuseppe Schino, Giuseppe Pasquine, Nicola
Muscente, Vincenzo Gazzillo
Recorded January 19, 1920

51   Italian American Sportsmen's Club, Inc.
Purposes: to promote and foster interest in gunning, hunting,
fishing; to conduct contests and meets; to create or assist in any worthy
charity or benevolence
Agent: Walter D. Cougle, 137 East State Street
Trustees: Flori Ercoli, Lorenzo Rossi, Louis Agrestini, Bartolino Rossi,
Arghesano Brillantini
Recorded February 7, 1921

52   *Nuova Societá Mutuo Soccorso Casteltermini*
Purposes: mutual aid and death benefit
Agent: Carmelo Severino, Camera's Hall, South Broad Street
Trustees: Carmelo Severino, Vincenzo Giuliani fu Vincenzo, Giuseppe
Pacera, Giuseppe Sciarrotta fu Silvestro, Giuseppe Midulla
Recorded May 16, 1921

53   *Societá di Mutuo Soccorso Ferentilese*
Purposes: beneficial
Agent: Melindo Persi, 485 Chestnut Avenue
Trustees: Melindo Persi, Michele Lerisini, Giulio Costandini, Beniamino

Scorsolino, Fulvio Ridolfi
Recorded June 14, 1921

54 *Societá di Mutuo Soccorso Favignana*
Purposes: mutual aid and death benefit
Agent: Biagio Mulé, 600 Whittaker Avenue
Trustees: Biagio Mulé, Angelo Mulé, Pietro Mercurio, Giovanni Bevilacqua, Francesco Rallo
Recorded July 1, 1921

55 Young Italian Social Club of South Trenton
Purposes: social and athletic
Agent: John Russo, 227 Asbury Ferry Street
Trustees: John Russo, Carl Ailey, Lawrence Fachelli, Vito Fuch, James Mahr
Recorded July 18, 1921

56 South Trenton Italian Association
Purposes: advancement of education; intellectual, social, and welfare of the Italians of Trenton, Mercer Co., and the State of New Jersey
Agent: Alexander De Rosa, 267 Hamilton Avenue
Trustees: Alex De Rosa, Jerry Conte, Angelo Fiore, Frank Santomeno, Frank Videtto, Rocco Angioletti
Recorded September 15, 1921

57 Villalba Citizens' Club of Trenton, N.J.
Purposes: furtherance of sociability, political science, recreation of its members
Agent: John Nalbone, 29 Nassau Street
Trustees: John Nalbone, Anthony Lauria, Sebastiano Castranovo, Vincenzo Sperazza, Peter W. Radice
Recorded August 7, 1922

58 *Circolo Filodrammatico Enrico Caruso di Trenton, N.J.*
Purposes: promotion of drama, literature, and art; fostering social and fraternal spirit among members
Agent: Matthew Di Nola, 93 Ferrier Street
Trustees: Matthew Di Nola, Querino De Santis, Nicola Paranzino, Calogero Di Pietro, Antonio Scalia
Recorded August 18, 1922

59 Italian Political Liberty Club of Trenton, N.J.
Purposes: to gather all American citizens of the Order Sons of Italy in America, and to promote the elevation of both the economical and political situation of its members throughout the state
Agent: Angelo Ruffo, 524 South Clinton Avenue
Trustees: Rocco Napoliello, Tommaso Di Filippo, Nicola Guida, Gaetano

San Filippo, Pasquale Lo Bue
Recorded October 17, 1922

60 Young Italian-American Social Club of North Trenton
Purposes: social, intellectual, recreative
Agent: Peter W. Radice, 86 Paul Avenue
Trustees: Peter W. Radice, Nick Famcell, Vincenzo Sperrazza, Tony Fiorello
Recorded November 21, 1922

61 *Circolo Filodrammatico Gabriele D'Annunzio di Trenton, N.J.*
Purposes: promotion of drama and the study of literature and art
Agent: Giuseppe Innammorato, 219 Cooper Street
Trustees: John Tartaglia, Nicola Giammari, Zulfrano Domenicantonio, Gioacchino Valeri, Primiano Lombardi
Recorded November 21, 1922

62 *Loggia Savoia* Emergency Association
Purposes: to render assistance to the *Loggia Operaia Savoia* No. 688 of the O.F.D.I. in all emergencies that may arise economically, socially, and educationally. The association is constituted only by members of the Loggia Operaia Savoia.
Agent: Angelo Ruffo, 524 South Clinton Avenue
Trustees: Anthony S. Rebecca, Frank Pricola, Giuseppe Chiantese, Giuseppe Marcantonio, Filippo D'Angelo
Recorded February 24, 1923

63 Mercer Social Club
Purposes: to promote social intercourse among the members, and to cultivate and improve the intellect by indulging in readings, speakings, and in other endeavors, and in entertainment and amusements
Agent: Angel Pellettieri, 15 West Lafayette Street
Trustees: Charles Keeler, John Purcell, James Cuparello, Oscar Pellettieri, Angel Pellettieri
Recorded March 19, 1923

64 *Circolo Umbro-Annarese di Trenton, N.J.*
Purposes: furtherance of the education of its members and others, and the promotion of friendly relations of its members
Agent: Settimio Bucchi, 132 Kent Street
Trustees: Enrico Angelucci, Settimio Bucchi, Francesco Sensi, Roberto Reali, Settimio Marciotti
Recorded April 3, 1923

65 Liberty Political Club of Trenton, N.J.
Purposes: to promote social, intellectual and fraternal fellowship among its members

Agent: Salvatore Scarlata, 32 George Street
Trustees: Salvatore Scarlata, Milo Lombardo, Raffaele Nalbone, Francesco Ferrara, Luigi Nalbone
Recorded July 23, 1923

66 Young Italian Social Club of the Ninth Ward
Purposes: to promote social and athletic activities among young Italians of the Ninth Ward
Agent: Charles Colucci, 544 South Clinton Avenue
Officers: Fritz Dileo, president; John Frascella, vice president; Charles Colucci, secretary; Charles Colucci, treasurer
Directors: Oscar Mancini, Jerry Tedeschi, Robert Critti, Joseph Dillon
Recorded October 26, 1923

67 *Associazione Nazionale ex Combattenti Italiani, Sezione di Trenton, N.J.*
Purposes: to cultivate and maintain a spirit of comradeship and fraternalism among male persons of Italian birth or extraction, such persons being veterans who were under the service of the Kingdom of Italy, either army or navy, in the recent world war.
Agent: Ignazio Sorce, 251 North Clinton Avenue
Trustees: Gaetano Liuzzo, Giuseppe Morreale, Calogero Frugale, Giuseppe D'Amico, Antonio Mirasola
Recorded February 20, 1924

68 Club *Cattolico Maria Santissima di Casandrino of Trenton, N.J.*
Purposes: educational, patriotic; promotion of the social welfare of its members
Agent: Severino Battista, St. Joachim's Hall
Trustees: Severino Battista, president; Nicola Di Mattia, secretary; Luigi Morelli, treasurer
Recorded March 12, 1924

69 *Circolo Filodrammatico Felice Cavallotti di Trenton, N.J.*
Purposes: social, moral, intellectual welfare of its members
Agent: Romildo Casciani, 712 Brunswick Avenue
Trustees: Quirino De Santis, Salvatore Bartoleschi, Luigi Massa, Nicola Paranzino, Joe Fogio
Recorded May 5, 1924

70 *Societá Femminile Villalba di M.S. di Trenton, N.J.*
Purposes: mutual aid and death benefit
Trustees: Maria Cammarata, Lucia Castello, Grazia Cammarata, Frances Immordino, Rosina Ippolito
Recorded May 20, 1924

71 International Social Club
Purposes: promotion of social and recreational activities in the community

Agent: Samuel Compy, 141 Fulton Street
Trustees: Samuel Compy, Julius Romani, Morris Rossi, Peter Epifanio, Charles Pelcz
Recorded December 1, 1924

72 Garibaldi Independent Political Club of Trenton, N.J.
Purposes: promotion of political, social, and civic welfare of its members; to instruct, aid and prepare its members in becoming naturalized citizens; provide lectures and social entertainment
Agent: Salvatore Caltagirone, 320 North Clinton Avenue
Trustees: Salvatore Caltagirone, Vincenzo Giuliano, Onofrio Calderone, Rosario Noto, Giuseppe De Carlo
Recorded January 14, 1925

73 *Societá Sacra Famiglia*
Purposes: to promote the Roman Catholic religion; to educate Italian children in the English and Italian languages, and to promote and advance their religious training, according to the tenets of the Roman Catholic Church
Agent: Calogero Plumeri, 39 Paul Avenue
Trustees: Calogero Muni, Calogero Immordino, Vincenzo Bonfanti, Giuseppe Pizza, Frank La Paglia, Calogero Plumeri, Filippo Mosca, Alfonso Plumeri
Recorded March 25, 1925

74 Bay Ridge Club
Purposes: social and recreational entertainment of its members
Agent: Charles Tschudin, 682 Stokes Avenue
Trustees: Charles Tschudin, Charles Chamberlain, Charles Compagnucci, Charles Nalbone, William Ritter
Recorded March 30, 1925

75 Chambersburg Recreation Club of Trenton, N.J.
Purposes: promotion of social welfare and athletic sports
Agent: Frank Cristiani, 16-18 Mott Street
Trustees: Frank Graziano, Thomas Tanzone, Anthony Weaver, Joseph Persico, Joseph Tanzone
Recorded October 27, 1925

76 Italian Welfare Association
Purposes: to collect, receive, disburse and distribute moneys, goods, wares, and merchandise of all kinds and descriptions for the purpose of helping and assisting persons who are in need of help, sustenance, and means of livelihood
Agent: Frank Russo, 571 Bellevue Avenue
Trustees: Frank Russo, Tito Salamandra, James P. Frey, John Manziano,

Attilio Perilli
Recorded November 6, 1925

77 *Operaia Savoia – Societá di M.S. di Trenton, N.J.*
Purposes: promotion of social, economical, and political welfare of its members; beneficial and patriotic; and for mutual aid
Agent: Angelo Ruffo, 522-524 South Clinton Avenue
Trustees: Giuseppe Santosuosso, Tommaso De Filippo, Frank Pricolo, Nicola Guida, Rocco Napoliello
Recorded November 23, 1925

78 *Societá di M.S. Stella D'Italia di Trenton, N.J.*
Purposes: mutual aid and death benefit
Agent: Salvatore Calá, 53 Paul Avenue
Trustees: Salvatore Moscarello, Amico Rosario, Salvatore Bentivenga
Recorded April 12, 1926

79 *Circolo Muratori Italiani*
Purposes: educational, intellectual; the welfare of its members
Agent: Erino Sebastiani, 770 Chambers Street
Trustees: Nicola Scozzari, Peter A. Pulone, Carmelo Cipolla
Recorded May 3, 1926

80 Cannara Social Club of Trenton, N.J.
Purposes: furtherance of sociability, intellectuality, and recreation of its members
Agent: Giuseppe Cuccagna, 202 Fulton Street
Trustees: Titi Torretti, Frank Graziano, Henry Cuccagna
Recorded October 23, 1926

81 Villalba Association Club of Trenton, N.J.
Purposes: social, intellectual, recreative
Agent: Joseph La Marca, 743 Brunswick Avenue
Trustees: Joseph La Marca, Rosario Vizzini, Joseph Nalbone, Charles Riggs, Vincenzo La Marca
Recorded December 11, 1926

82 *Circolo Sportivo Italiano*
Purposes: all kinds of sports; beneficial welfare of its members
Agent: Nichola Farinella, 47 Paul Avenue
Trustees: James Fruscione, Ignazio Sorce, Michael Cammarata, John Farinella, Giuseppe Fruscione
Recorded December 14, 1926

83 *Societá Sorelle Monteleonesi di M.S. of Trenton, N.J.*
Purposes: health benefits, death benefits
Agent: Rose Bella, 418 Hudson Street

Trustees: Rose Bella, president; Lina C. Bianchi, vice president; Santina Radice, secretary; Jennie Sereni, vice secretary; Antonia Venanzi, treasurer
Recorded April 16, 1927

84 Italian-American Workmen's Club
Purposes: social and educational advancement of its members
Agent: Joseph R. Petrino, 527 Chestnut Avenue
Trustees: Tony Colucci, Paolo Bernabei, Luigi Filipponi, Nicholas Povia, Bigomi Primo, Pietro Braconi, Pasquale Paglione, Michele Coiante
Recorded May 24, 1927

85 *Circolo Educativo Pugliese*
Purposes: promotion of social, economical, and political welfare of its members; mutual aid for its members
Agent: Giuseppe Adduci, 312 Hudson Street
Trustees: Gabriele Battisti, Giuseppe Adduci, Angelo Povio, Giuseppe Grammatico, Luigi Fabiani
Recorded June 23, 1927

86 Casteltermini Citizens' Club of Trenton, N.J.
Purposes: social, educational, political; promotion of friendship among members
Agent: Domenick Ciccone, 15 Tyrell Avenue
Trustees: Domenick Ciccone, Gaetano Liuzzo, Vincenzo Mangione, Giuseppe Ottobre, Joseph Mainiero
Recorded September 22, 1928

87 *Societá Femminile Ferentilese di M.S.*
Purposes: mutual aid and death benefit
Agent: Ninetta Orsi, 1024 Chambers Street
Trustees: Ada Rossi, Clementina Costantini, Irma Ferri, Clara Torlini, Florence Agabiti
Recorded August 11, 1928

88 *Societá Casteltermini di M.S.*
Purposes: mutual aid and death benefit
Agent: Michele Formicola, 418 Hudson Street
Trustees: Sigismondo Fantauzzo, Michele Formicola, Gaetano Sanfilippo, Gaetano Pellitteri, Antonio Scannella
Recorded October 11, 1928

89 *Grande Corte Giovanni Bovio No. 1 F.O. di M.S.*
Purposes: benevolent, social; welfare society of the Italian people residing in the State of New Jersey
Agent: Henry Ezzo, 423 Lamberton Street

Trustees: Henry Ezzo, Pasquale Panaro, Emilio A. Di Donato, Luigi Coltre, Antonio Calabrese
Recorded October 19, 1928

90 *Italia Riunita Societa' di M.S.*
Purposes: mutual aid and death benefit
Agent: Melindo Persi, 487 Chestnut Avenue
Trustees: Natale Coltre, John Fileni, Pietro Bonanni, Luigi Scartocci, Frank Aloisi
Recorded September 23, 1929

91 North Trenton Italian Democratic Club
Purposes: social and political
Agent: Giuseppe Colletti, 32 George Street
Trustees: Giuseppe Colletti, Raffaele Nalbone, Giuseppe Schillacci
Recorded October 25, 1929

92 Ferry Athletic Association
Purposes: promotion of athletics and social activities among its members
Agent: Louis Ferry, 201 Hudson Street
Trustees: James Gantiosa, Louis Ferry, Anthony Mituri, Joseph Smisson, Armond Conti
Recorded April 19, 1930

93 The Italian G.O.P. League of Mercer County
Purposes: political, educational, benevolent
Agent: Peter A. Spair, 340 Hamilton Avenue
Trustees: Lew Angelo, James R. Marolda, Daniel A. Dileo, Peter A. Spair, Dr. Anthony Lettiere, Fred J. Pone, Pasquale Dileo
Recorded October 9, 1930

94 Young Italian-American Club of North Trenton
Purposes: to unite the young Italians by birth or parentage to bring about a better social standing, and educating them in their civic duty
Agent: Joseph Plumeri, S.E. Corner Paul and Nassau Streets
Trustees: Charles J. Mune, Joseph Castranovo, Peter W. Radice, Louis Valenza, Isidore Di Stefano, Nick Ferrara, Angelo Lupo, Joseph Plumeri
Recorded November 20, 1930

95 Italian Democratic League of Mercer County
Purposes: to promote good fellowship, mutual aid, and cooperation with other leagues of the same party; to conduct charitable, social affairs; to assist in making new citizens; to advance the interest of the Democratic Party
Agent: Carl J. Maiorino, 612 South Clinton Avenue

Trustees: Carl J. Maiorino, Thomas H. Lettiere, Michael A. Pesce, Gaetano E. Caiazzo, Anthony S.D. Rebecca, Samuel Naples, Joseph C. Guidotti, Amedeo Ciabattoni, Melindo Persi
Recorded January 5, 1931

96   Mott Social Club of Trenton, N.J.
Purposes: social and intellectual welfare of its members
Agent: Fritz Dileo, 16-18 Mott Street
Trustees: Fritz Dileo, Pasquale Chianese, James Formica, Anthony W. Rinaldi, John Radice
Recorded June 4, 1931

97   *Dr. Cav. Giuseppe Pantaleone di M.S. di Trenton, N.J.*
Purposes: to pay sick and death benefits
Agent: Vincenzo Fiorello, 15 Dexter Street
Trustees: Giuseppe Farina, Vincenzo Fiorello, Luigi Amico, Vincenzo Cacciatore, Onofrio Schillacci, Giuseppe Guarino, John Ferrara, Calogero D'Amico
Recorded June 5, 1931

98   North Trenton Italian Republican Club
Purposes: political, non-profit
Agent: Rosalino Guarino, 53 E. Paul Avenue
Trustees: Rosalino Guarino, Anthony Fiorello, John Ferrara, Vincenzo Fiorello, Frank La Paglia, Albert Di Maria, Luisa Immordino, Vincenzo Cacciatore
Recorded July 3, 1931

99   The Supreme Lodge of the Amici of America
Purposes: to unite in bonds of friendship American citizens of Italian birth, origin, or descent; to encourage the highest cultural attainments, awaken to the fullest measure the initiative and genius of the Italian race in America, reduce racial barriers to a sympathetic understanding; health and death benefits
Agent: Joseph J. Felcone, 717 Broad St. National Bank Building
Trustees: Nicholas Albano, Salvatore F. La Corte, Joseph J. Busichio, Thomas F. Vigorito, Joseph J. Felcone
Recorded October 1, 1931

100   Fifth Ward Gunning Club
Purposes: activities and good sportsmanship in fishing and gunning
Agent: Levi J. Blizard, 54 Bond Street
Trustees: Levi J. Blizard, Tony De Marco, Nick Dippoliti, Mark Berardi, Anthony Di Pulla
Recorded October 13, 1931

101   North Trenton Athletic Association Club

Purposes: social purpose
Agent: Charles Castella, 34 George Street
Trustees: Charles Castella, Angelo La Marca, Louis Vasta, Joseph Vizzini, Blacey Farino
Recorded October 13, 1931

102   Fifth Ward Italian American Democratic Club
Purposes: political and social
Agent: Domenic D'Amico, 286 Northk Clinton Avenue
Trustees: Domenic D'Amico, Nick Midulla, Giuseppe Pellitteri, Michelangelo Modica, Arthur Sciarrotta
Recorded January 28, 1932

103   Roebling Avenue Democratic Club
Purposes: to espouse the principles of the Democratic Party and to develop social and athletic activity in the community
Agent: Frank Burkus, 767 Roebling Avenue
Trustees: Alfonso Spera, Frank Kovacs, Ralph Tuccillo, Frank Sensi, Alfonso Serpico
Recorded April 16, 1932

104   Italian Club
Purposes: furtherance of the education of its members and others; promotion of friendly and social relations of its members; social entertainment
Agent: Patsy Maggi, 340 Hamilton Avenue
Trustees: Steve Faggella, Patsy Maggi, Daniel Brenna, Vincent Caputi, Vito Brenna
Recorded September 7, 1932

105   Elmer Athletic Associaton Social Club
Purposes: social, athletic, baseball, and basketball
Agent: Daniel Petry, 213 Elmer Street
Trustees: Daniel Petry, Michael Petry, Marco Battiste, Carmin Ecalella, Nicholas Migliacci
Recorded September 9, 1932

106   Bilardo Athletic Association Social Club
Purposes: social, athletic, baseball and basketball
Agent: Pasquale Bilardo, 218 South Clinton Avenue
Trustees: Pasquale Bilardo, Sossio Bencivengo, Louis Sorento, Frank Di Matteo, Frank Della Rossa
Recorded December 23, 1932

107   Italian American Independent League
Purposes: political, social, entertaining, civic
Agent: Anthony S.D. Rebecca, 8 Hollywood Avenue

Trustees: Joseph Formica, Otto Marzulli, Henry Commini, Anthony Invidiato, John Frascella
Recorded June 17, 1933

108   Agabiti Athletic Association
Purposes: to promote athletics and good fellowship among members
Agent: Joe De Marco, 710 Roebling Avenue
Trustees: Michael Tott, John Giori, William Giori, Joseph De Marco, Joseph Salvatore
Recorded July 6, 1933

109   Butler Athletic Association and Social Club
Purposes: social, entertaining, and athletic: baseball, basketball, and football
Agent: Carl Perlo, 713 Whittaker Avenue
Trustees: William Povia, Paul Migliacci, Louis Quisito, Frank Di Vietro, Julius Pozzi
Recorded July 18, 1933

110   Roman Social Club
Purposes: athletic, social, and civic
Agent: Libro Bonanni, 139 Morris Avenue
Trustees: Anthony Caracciolo, Anthony Franco, Clement Lanzi, Dominic Palmiere, Libro Bonanni
Recorded September 6, 1933

111   North Trenton Italian-American Social Club
Purposes: to engage in recreational, educational, and social activities; to inculcate a deeper interest in civic responsibilities and political duties as good citizens
Agent: Pasquale Daloisio, 1281 Princeton Avenue
Trustees: Camillo Masciovecchio, Ciriaco Daloisio, John Ciricola, John Gregorio
Recorded October 19, 1933

112   *Societá Femminile M.S. Casteltermini di Trenton, N.J.*
Purposes: educational, beneficial, patriotic; relief for its members
Agent: Elvira Stella, 42 Tyrell Avenue
Trustees: Grazia Palmieri, Vincenzina Sciarrotta, Elvira Stella, Lucia Castello, Maria Faldetta
Recorded December 13, 1933

113   Italian-American Bocce Club of Trenton, N.J.
Purposes: promotion of social and sporting events among its members, having for its major scope, the development in this community the Italian game of Bocce
Agent: Frank Landolfi, 47 Butler Street

Trustees: Leonard Tartaglia, Nicola Guida, Frank Pricolo, Joseph Sacchitelli, Frederick Travis
Recorded January 23, 1934

114   Italian Benevolent League
Purposes: to provide food, clothing, shelter, legal and medical aid to the less fortunate deserving of such assistance without charge; to promote good citizenship; to protect civil rights of the people in the community; and to promote good fellowship
Agent: Carl J. Maiorino, 146 Hamilton Avenue
Trustees: Carl J. Maiorino, Dr. George A. Corio, Raphael Petito
Recorded March 8, 1934

115   Ninth Ward Italian Social Club
Purposes: social benefits and developments; to develop the welfare of its members for education; to promote civic purposes
Agent: Gaetano Chiacchio, 303 1/2 Hudson Street
Trustees: Victor Silvestri, Anthony Morelli, Gaetano Chiacchio, Andrea De Vito, Silvestro Morabito, Domenico Ferrante, Vincenzo Mauceri
Recorded May 8, 1934

116   *Boccistico Coloniale* Club
Purposes: to promote social, fraternal, and athletic activities for the benefit of its members; to promote the general welfare for its members
Agent: Adelino Conti, 23 Davis Street
Trustees: Archesano Brillantini, Egisto Massoli, John Fratticcioli, Galliano Scaccetti, Adelmo Conti
Recorded June 15, 1934

117   The Richard D. La Guardia Association, Inc.
Purposes: to persuade and encourage Richard D. La Guardia to enter the campaign for city commissioner of Trenton in 1935
Agent: Albert A. Ripman, 137 E. State Street
(Among) Trustees: Michael A. Pesce, Dr. O.D. Guglielmelli, Frank L. Cellini, Joseph H. Manze
Recorded June 20, 1934

118   *Nuova Casteltermini* Social Club
Purposes: to promote sociability, welfare, education, morality
Agent: Placido Mule', 216 North Clinton Avenue
Trustees: Joseph Plumeri, Carmelo Severino, Vincenzo Giuliano, Giuseppe Pellitteri
Recorded August 25, 1934

119   Italian Republican League of Chambersburg
Purposes: social and political
Agent: Rocco F. Pagano, 314 Elmer Street

Trustees: Nicholas Ciliento, Giacomo Caiazzo, Rocco F. Pagano, Raffaele Giordano, Vitaliano Ciliento
Recorded November 26, 1934

120 Chambersburg Hunting Club
Purposes: to promote good fellowship among all interested in fishing and hunting; to respect the fishing and hunting laws; to establish and maintain higher degree of efficiency among members
Agent: Nicholas Congiundi, 183 Division Street
Trustees: Nicholas Congiundi, Francis J. Black, Charles Congiundi, Philip J. Crecco, Joseph H. Franks
Recorded February 21, 1935

121 Grand Lodge of the State of New Jersey, Independent Order Sons of Italy
Purposes: a secret, fraternal order of persons of Italian birth or origin, of good moral character; social well-being; health and death benefits
Agent: Angelo Ruffo, 41 Bayard Street
Trustees: Angelo Ruffo, Michele Pesce, Angelo Ciccolella (only those from Trenton listed here)
Recorded May 14, 1935

122 *Circolo Filodrammatico Coloniale*
Purposes: to perform all kinds of plays, comedy sketches, for the benefit of society; to promote social welfare among its members
Agent: Antonio Morelli, 305 Hudson Street
Trustees: Joseph Marrazzo, Agostino Di Giuseppe, Antonio Morelli, Michele D'Addio, Giuseppe Pica
Recorded May 27, 1935

123 *Roma* Civic League of Trenton, N.J.
Purposes: to inspire patriotism, promote good government, inculcate democracy, foster social and recreative activities
Agents: George Calisti, John Manganelli, 420 Hudson Street
Trustees: George Calisti, Cesare Orsi, Sylvester Stella, John Benedetti, John Manganelli
Recorded June 4, 1935

124 Italian-American Civic League of Trenton, N.J.
Purposes: civic, social, educational
Agent: John A. Ragazzo, Corner Mott and Hudson Streets
Trustees: John A. Ragazzo, Maurice S. Persi, John Cristofani, Gennaro Cardelia, Girard Perugino
Recorded July 29, 1935

125 The Unity League
Purposes: to promote and disseminate the principles of government

in the United States; to build up a good citizenry; to participate in political, civic, and social activities
Office: 406 South Clinton Avenue
Trustees; Dr. Charles Cella, James Fuccello, Frank Di Giuseppe, Henry Commini, Nicholas Dondiego
Recorded July 31, 1935

126 Chestnut Social Club
Purposes: social, intellectual, recreative
Agent: Salvatore Guido, 487 Chestnut Avenue
Trustees: Alexander Misticoni, Mario D'Abronzo, William Stanzione, Salvatore Guido, Arthur Masino
Recorded September 13, 1935

127 Colonial Catholic Club Maria SS. di Casandrino of Trenton, N.J.
Purposes: educational, patriotic; promotion of social welfare of its members
Agent: Salvatore D'Angelo, 1004 Quinton Avenue
Trustees: Salvatore D'Angelo, Angelo Povio, Gennaro D'Angelo, Nicola Chianese, Filippo Rinaldo
Recorded October 7, 1935

128 *Entente Cordiale* Social Club
Purposes: to promote and foster good will and friendship among members
Agent: Frank Martino, 314 Elmer Street
Witnesses: Joseph Belardo, John Russo, Henry Tallone, Pasquale Di Cola, Joseph Giangrasso
Recorded November 9, 1935

129 Washington Social Club of Chambersburg
Purposes: social activities, friendship among members
Agent: Michael Mancuso, 132 Bayard Street
Trustees: Michael Mancuso, John Territo, Anthony Ricigliano, Joseph Capodici
Recorded December 9, 1935

130 Rosemont Social Club
Purposes: intellectual, civic; sports; non-political
Agent: Angelo Crea, 324 Emory Avenue
Trustees: Angelo Crea, Charles Chianese, Joseph Guano, Pasquale D'Amico, Louis Migliaccio
Recorded January 25, 1936

131 Fourth Ward Young Democratic Club, Inc.
Purposes: to stimulate in young people an active interest in governmental affairs; to increase efficiency of popular government; to

perpetuate the ideals and principles of the Democratic Party; to provide for the people the highest degree of justice and social welfare.
Agent: Donald De Marco, 243 Lamberton Street
Trustees: Francis Caperello, Vito A. Fuch, Donald De Marco, Frank Bruno, Fudio De Core
Recorded July 2, 1936

132   Chambersburg Young Republican Club
Purposes: social and political
Agent: Gerard Radice, Corner Roebling and Washington Streets
Trustees: Joseph J. De Puglio, William Povia, Gerard Radice, Frank Limone, Michael De Puglio
Recorded August 29, 1936

133   Fourth Ward Independent Romans Social Club
Purposes: social affairs, dances, and parties
Agent: John Fiore, 407 Bridge Street
Trustees: Agusto Mattozzi, Vincenzo Carrocci, Angelo Angelini
Recorded August 31, 1936

134   National Independent Order Sons of Italy
Purposes: as stated earlier
Agent: Angelo Ruffo, 41 Bayard Street
Trustees: (only those from Trenton listed here) Angelo Ruffo, Michele Pesce, Angelo Ciccolella, Erasmo S. Ciccolella, Salvatore Ciccolella
Recorded March 25, 1936

135   *Societá Femminile Romana di M.S.*
Purposes: health and death benefits
Agent: Lavinia Bella and Ada Corsalini, Casteltermini Hall, Hudson Street
Trustees: Lavinia Bella, Delfina Luisini, Lina. B. Eleuteri, Clelia Pierleonardi, Ada Corsalini
Recorded October 13, 1936

136   Italian-American World War Veterans Association
Purposes: to form an association of World War veterans of Italian extraction who have served under the American flag; to promote the civic, commercial, industrial betterment of its members; to take part in any meritorious movement for the general good
Agent: Dominic De Felice, 63 Butler Street
Trustees: Dominic De Felice, Michael Ferrante, Attilio Cortesini, Andrew Sivo, Felix Pacilio, Fred Zavaglia, Joe S. Fradusco
Recorded October 22, 1936

137   Casino Social Club of Trenton, N.J.
Purposes: social and athletic

Agent: August Di Giuseppe, 323 Elmer Street
Trustees: Nicasio Cipriano, Stephen Piraino, Luke Bencivengo, Pat Chianese, Domenic D. Ciaramella, August Di Giuseppe
Recorded December 14, 1936

138 Social Political Club *Friulano*
Purposes: to promote citizenship; educational, patriotic; to promote social welfare of its members
Agent: Angelo Santin, 332 Cummings Avenue
Trustees: Angelo Santin, Risieri Pez, Pietro Bertolini, Luigi Fantin, Erminio Zampeze, Anthony Fantin, Olimpio Bidinost, Erminio Vivian
Recorded March 18, 1937

139 Lamberton Street Independent Social Club
Purposes: social and political
Agent: Calogero Piraino, 613 Lamberton Street
Trustees: Thomas Nalbone, Joseph Abarno, Benny Amato, William Rodenwald, Calogero Piraino
Recorded November 30, 1937

140 *Societá di M.S. Maresciallo Pietro Badoglio*
Purposes: health and death benefits
Agent: Agostino Butticé, Casteltermini Hall, 420 Hudson Street
Trustees: Filippo Rinaldi, Vincenzo Ialello, Pietro Ponzio
Recorded January 19, 1938

141 *Circolo Coloniale Italiano*
Purposes: educational, patriotic; promotion of social welfare of its members
Agent: Antonio D'Angelo, 418 Elmer Street
Trustees: Angelo Povio, Antonio D'Angelo, Giuseppe Femiano, Antonio Morelli, Pietro Verde
Recorded May 26, 1938

142 Piraino Social Club
Purposes: social, educational
Agent: Calogero Piraino, 613 Lamberton Street
Trustees: Calogero Piraino, Ben Amato, William Rodenwald, Michael Vaniska, Armando Onorati
Recorded June 28, 1938

143 Italian Cultural Club
Purposes: to promote intellectual, moral, and physical development, and the social welfare of its members; to help its members in every manner possible
Agent: Gaetano Pagliaro, 911 Chambers Street
Trustees: Gaetano Pagliaro, Stephen Faggello, Paolo Bacchini

Recorded February 23, 1939

144 North Trenton Republican Civic League
Purposes: to disseminate information pertaining to governmental activities; to encourage and develop interest in civic affairs of the community; to promote good fellowship and the mutual assistance of its members
Agent: Anthony Liccardo, 38 Wainwright Avenue
Trustees: Anthony Liccardo, James Martorana, Leo N. Ullrich, Chris Stinger, Dante Bambo
Recorded May 4, 1939

145 *Societá di M.S. Umberto di Savoia*
Purposes: to provide sick and death benefits; to provide and encourage social activity among its members; to teach the principles of good citizenship to make its members better and more useful
citizens of these United States
Agent: Mario H. Volpe, Room 401, 150 E. State Street
Trustees: Davide C. Ronca, V. Michele Tozzi, Giuseppe Faminani, James Corio, Domenico Buchicchio
Recorded August 2, 1939

146 The Roman Beneficial Society changed its name to *Societá Romana di M.S.*
Sylvester Stella, president; Luigi Di Marco, secretary
Recorded September 21, 1939

147 Marconi Catholic Men's Club
Purposes: social welfare, friendship among its members
Agent: Anthony J. Radice, 47 College Street
Trustees: Anthony J. Radice, Frank A. Carmignani, Anthony Dragonetti, Joseph G. Mumolie, James A. Mumolie
Recorded January 9, 1940

148 Trenton A.C. Social Club
Purposes: social and athletic
Agent: Arthur Coluccio, 46 Jefferson Street
Trustees: George Persichetti, William W. Grieb, Arthur Colucci, Louis Persichetti, Andrew Erick
Recorded January 10, 1940

149 Trenton Post No. 2 – Italian-American World War Veterans of the U.S., Inc.
Purposes: to uphold and defend the Constitution, preserve memories, inculcate a sense of obligation to the nation; to promote peace
Agent: Joseph Bella, 241 Hamilton Avenue
Trustees: James Esposti, Morris Totory, Bernardino Viola, Joseph Bella,

Charles Compagnucci
Recorded January 24, 1940

150 Roman Social Club of Chambersburg
Purposes: to promote friendlier feelings and social contact among the
younger element of Italian extraction
Agent: Santi Mirabelli, Cor. Whittaker Avenue and Butler Street
Trustees: Adolfo Pontani, Domenick Oliveri, Santi Mirabelli, Ernest
Paccillo, Joseph Bevilacqua
Recorded February 17, 1940

151 *Societá di Sant'Antonio di Padova*
Purposes: to develop interest in religion, assist one another, foster
education, assist in doing social work of all kinds, and develop
friendliness and kindliness between members
Agent: Gaetana Turano, 600 Whittaker Avenue
Trustees: Gaetana Turano, Raffaele Aiello, Fannie Longo, Mary
Maiurio, Frances Ammirato, Carrie Azzinaro
Recorded April 26, 1940

152 New Italian American Social Club, Inc.
Purposes: to help, encourage, and improve the welfare of the members;
to promote good government; to promote social and recreative
activities
Agent: Joseph Bilancio, 52 Mott Street
Trustees: Michael Campo, William Cacciatore, Joseph Bilancio,
Bernardino Viola, Mariano Lascari
Recorded August 29, 1940

153 North Trenton Athletic Club
Purposes: all kinds of sporting activities
Agent: Samuel Galardo, 76 East Paul Avenue
Trustees: Samuel Galardo, Benny La Penna, Joseph Favata, Joseph
Plumeri, Charles Tramantana
Recorded January 29, 1941

154 Princeton Social Club of Trenton, N.J.
Purposes: to bring together a group of young men to establish good
fellowship and to encourage discussion of civic problems of our
community
Agent: Christopher Garruba, 51 Chase Street
Trustees: Ralph Di Memmo, Herman Oliveri, Christopher Garruba,
Samuel Ferrara, Louis Alu
Recorded January 31, 1941

155 Ninth and Tenth Ward Social Club of Trenton, N.J.
Purposes: social

Agent: August Marshall, 147 Mott Street
Trustees: August Marshall, Louis Marcello, Michael Capone, Anthony
Angelene, Anthony Badessa
Recorded June 20, 1941

Following are lists of organized groups appearing in sources other than the papers of incorporation.

In the *Trenton Times* and the *Trenton Evening Times*

1   Adelaide Cairoli, Order Sons of Italy
2   Atlas Girls' Club
3   Atlas Progressive Club
4   Baron A.A.
5   Bayard Social Club
6   Butler Youths
7   Chambersburg Business and Professional Women
8   Chambersburg Republican Club
9   Colonial League
10 Colonial Social Club
11 Columbus Civic League (formerly Italian-American Civic League)
12 Columbus Lodge, Order Sons of Italy
13 Columbus Women's Welfare League
14 Cristoforo Social Club
15 Damselettes
16 Debonair Girls
17 Ever Ready Club
18 Galileo Science Society
19 Giovanni Bovio Mutual Aid Benefit Society
20 Italian-American Independent Club
21 Italian-American Independent Club of North Trenton
22 Italian-American Ladies' Social Club
23 Italian-American League of Mercer County
24 Italian Social Service Center
25 Italian-American Veterans of the World War
26 Italian-American Women's Welfare Committee
27 Italian-American Young Republicans
28 Italian Business and Professional Men's Club
29 Italian Federation of Mercer County
30 Joy Club
31 Kent A.A.
32 Kent Camp No. 49, Woodmen of the World
33 Ladies' Auxiliary of North Trenton Italian-American Social Club
34 Ladies' Auxiliary of Trenton Post No. 2, Italian-American World War
      Veterans

35   Laff-a-Lot Girls' Club
36   Loggia South Trenton, Order Sons of Italy
37   Maddalena Carioni Lodge, Order Sons of Italy
38   Marconi Catholic Young Men's Club
39   Master Social Club
40   Melrose Club
41   Mercer County Committee of Loyal American Women
42   Model Social Club
43   New Colonial Dramatic Club
44   Old Guard Club
45   Onyx Club
46   Pantaleone Lodge, Order Sons of Italy
47   Professional Women's Committee of the Civic League
48   Regina Marguerita Society
49   *Roma* Civic League
50   Seventh Ward Democratic Club
51   *Societá Nuova Stella d'Italia*
52   *Societá Nuova Stella Villalba Femminile*
53   *Societá San Michele, congrega San Gioacchino*
54   South Trenton Lodge, Order Sons of Italy
55   South Trenton Women's Social Club
56   Sportswoman Club
57   Trenton Lodge, Order Sons of Italy
58   Trenton Service Men's Committee
59   Tuesday Afternoon Card Club
60   Unico Club of Trenton
61   Usher's Society of Saint Joachim's Church
62   Young Democrats of Mercer County

In the Labor News
1   The Italian Culture Circle

In John S. Merzbacher's *Trenton's Foreign Colonies*
1   The Busy Bees (Girls)
2   The Educational Circle
3   The Junior Christian Endeavor Society
4   The Young Men's League of Mutual Aid
5   The Young Peoples Society of Christian Endeavor
All part of the Immanual Presbyterian Church

In the Minutes of the Trenton Board of Education
1   *Circolo Filodrammatico Casteltermini*
2   Committee of Loyal Americans of Italian Extraction
3   Fruscione Steers

 4 Italian Catholic Club
 5 Italian Citizen's League
 6 Italian Colonial Committee
 7 Italian Social Club
 8 Italian-American Club
 9 National Italian World War Veterans Assn.
10 Radice Star Teams
11 Recine A.C.
12 Ridolfi A.C.
13 Rossi's B.B. Team
14 Saint Joachim's A.C.
15 Social Women's Club
16 *Societá San Tammaro Femminile*
17 Trionfetti's Aces
18 United Italian Societies
19 Venanzi A.C.
20 Young Italian-American A.C.
21 Young Italian-American Social Club

In the records of St. Joachim's Church

 1 Christian Mothers
 2 *Congregazione di San Gioacchino*
 3 Daughters of Mary
 4 Holy Name Society
 5 Parochial Club
 6 Saint Joachim's Dramatic Club
 7 Saint Lucy Filippini Society
 8 Society of Saint Louis
 9 Young Ladies' Sodality
10 Young Men's League

In the records of Saint James R.C. Church

 1 Catholic Girls' Club
 2 Holy Name Society
 3 Holy Rosary Society
 4 New Society of the Holy Redeemer
 5 Saint Anne Society
 6 Saint Gabriel Society
 7 Saint Joseph Society
 8 Saint Lucy Filippini Society
 9 San Calogero Society
10 Young Ladies' Sodality

Where They Met

When Italian Americans first began to come together in groups such as the organizations which started to spring up in the 1880s, they had no meeting places of their own. As we have seen, Trenton was home to over 250 organizations of all types, almost all of which had no meeting places which they owned. As a result, most organizations made use of general purpose halls or of those owned by groups such as the Hibernians.

After the *Loggia Operaia Savoia* was incorporated in 1919, the members very soon took steps to buy a building where they could hold their meetings and social affairs. The Savoy Lodge was open every evening for those who came for conversation or card games. In addition, the members had a place where they could hold their annual banquets. The hall was rented for dances, parties, or wedding receptions.

The following list contains the names of the meeting places most frequently mentioned in newspaper announcements. It is interesting to note that, with but few exceptions, most of the meeting places were near the enclaves where the Italian Americans lived.

1 Anchak's Hall - 841-843 South Broad Street
2 Caiazzo's Hall - 518-522 South Clinton Avenue
3 Camera's Hall - 205 South Broad Street
4 Carroll Robbins School Auditorium - Tyler Street
5 Casa Monteleonese - Roebling Avenue and Franklin Street
6 Casteltermini Hall - Corner Hudson and Mott Streets
7 Columbus Hall - 551 South Clinton Avenue
8 Eagle Hall - 714 South Clinton Avenue
9 Hibernian Hall - 132 North Warren Street
10 Hildebrecht Hotel - West State Street
11 Hungarian Hall - Genesee Street and Hudson Street
12 International Institute - Corner South Clinton Avenue and Beatty Street
13 Italian-American Sportsmen's Club - Kuser Road
14 Junior High School No. 2 Auditorium - Gladstone Avenue
15 Liederkranz Hall - 1029 South Clinton Avenue
16 Nardi's Hall - Corner Emory and Whittaker Avenues
17 Padderatz Hall - 703 Whittaker Avenue
18 Roman Hall - Whittaker Avenue
19 Saint James R.C. Church Hall - East Paul Avenue
20 Saint Joachim's Church Hall - Bayard Street
21 Savoy Hall - 522-524 South Clinton Avenue

22   Stacy-Trent Hotel - West State Street
23   Trenton Central High School Auditorium - Chambers Street
24   Trenton High School Auditorium - Hamilton and Chestnut Avenues
25   Villalba Hall - 31 George Street
26   War Memorial Building - West Lafayette Street and John Fitch Way
27   New Washington School Auditorium - Emory Avenue
28   Old Washington School Auditorium

La scampagnata, i.e., the outing or picnic, was a favorite activity of the immigrants in their homeland; it was no less an enjoyable and pleasant pastime for them in their new land. They would prepare the same foods that would be enjoyed at home: macaroni with ragú, meatballs and links of sausage, chicken, loaves of crunchy bread, and lots of fruit. For the adults there were conversation, games of cards, and bocce. For the children great fun came from exploring the grounds, playing hide and go seek, and baseball. Though some families planned their own picnics, most took advantage of the picnics sponsored by societies or by the churches.

For these outings and picnics there were a few preferred locations:

Compy's Cozy Camp
Duck's Farm - in Ewing Township
Eggerts Crossing
Frank Chunko's Farm - Groveville Road
Henry's Grove - Eggerts Road
Plaag's Grove
Italian-American Sportsmen's Club - Kuser Road
Sullivan Grove - Washington Crossing Park

One may get a far better understanding of where the Italian Americans met and of how active they were if one combs the minutes of the Trenton Board of Education, where all groups renting gymnasiums, auditoriums, or grounds are listed. Unfortunately, one learns only that there was to be entertainment or a meeting or a lecture; rarely does one get as much information as "Armistice Day Program". When inquiries were made at the Administration Building about specifics, one learned that all application forms, which do list specifically the nature of the activity to be held, are routinely permitted to be destroyed every 10 years.

The items that follow are from the minutes of the Trenton Board of Education. Italian American groups began taking advantage of the schools' rooms, gymnasiums, and auditoriums in the late 1920s.

The first date given denotes the date of entry in the minutes.

May 1, 1919. Garibaldi Lodge No. 102 I.O.O.F. to use auditorium and gymnasium of the Robbins School the evening of May 10.

The Adelaide Cairoli Lodge (Italian women) to use the gymnasium of the Robbins School the evening of June 4.

October 2, 1919. The Order Sons of Italy to use the auditorium in the High School, the evening of October 5.

St. Joachim's Church to use rooms in the Hewitt School on Sundays from 10 to 12 a.m.

June 3, 1926. The Young Italian American Social Club to use athletic field Thursday evenings and Saturday afternoons beginning May 29.

November 4, 1926. Italian Citizen's League to use the Trenton High School auditorium December 2.

February 3, 1927. The Independent Order Sons of Italy to use the Trenton High School auditorium February 5 for a mass meeting.

May 8, 1927. The *Circolo Italiano di Trenton* to use the high school auditorium for a meeting May 8.

December 1, 1927. The Italian Catholic Club to use the Franklin School gymnasium Thursday evenings, beginning November 17.

October 4, 1928. The National Italian World War Veterans Association to use the high school auditorium November 11 for an Armistice Day Program.

November 1, 1928. The Italian Catholic Club to use the Franklin School gymnasium on Friday evenings for season games of basketball.

Request of the International Institute of the Y.W.C.A. for the free use of a room in the McClellan School on Tuesday afternoons and evenings for the purpose of conducting social and educational clubs for Italian girls and women.

January 12, 1931. The Trenton Unico Club to use the high school auditorium for a lecture on December 28.

July 2, 1931. The Young Italian American Athletic Club to use the Junior High School No. 1 athletic field Wednesday evenings and alternate Saturday afternoons.

November 5, 1931. The Kent Athletic Assn. to use the Junior High School No. 4 gymnasium Wednesday evenings beginning November 18 for basketball games.

The United Italian Societies to use the Junior High School No. 4 auditorium for Columbus Day Exercises on October 11.

July 7, 1932. The Sons and Daughters of Italy to use the Robbins School auditorium for a meeting on June 19.

December 1, 1932. The Agabiti Athletic Club to use gymnasium Monday evenings beginning November 28.

February 1, 1934. The United Lodges, Sons of Italy, to use the high school auditorium February 21 for entertainment.

June 7, 1934. The Italian Federation of Mercer County to use the high school auditorium May 20 for a meeting.

October 4, 1934. The Italian Federation of Mercer County to use the high school auditorium October 14 for a Columbus Day Celebration.

December 6, 1934. St. Joachim's Athletic Club to use the Franklin School auditorium Thursday evenings beginning in December for games.

February 7, 1935. The Madonna of Casandrino Society to use the high school auditorium April 11 for entertainment.

May 2, 1935. The Madonna of Casandrino Society to use high school auditorium May 31 for entertainment.

The Italian Federation of Mercer County to use high school auditorium May 24 for entertainment.

June 6, 1935. The Camera Dancing Studio to use the Robbins School auditorium June 1 for dance recital.

The Old Guard Club to use the high school auditorium May 3 for entertainment.

September 5, 1935. The Italian Christian Church to use the Centennial School grounds July 20 to August 31 for open-air meetings.

St. Joachim's Church to use the Centennial School grounds September 7 to 9 for dance.

November 7, 1935. the *Circolo Filodrammatico Casteltermini* to use high school auditorium December 15 for entertainment.

December 6, 1935. Trenton Post Italian War Veterans to use high school auditorium November 17 for entertainment.

Federation of Italian World War Veterans to use the high school auditorium November 30 for entertainment.

June 4, 1936. The Italian Red Cross Committee to use the high school auditorium June 7 for celebration.

September 3, 1936. The Italian American World War Veterans Assn. to use the high school auditorium September 4 for entertainment.

November 5, 1936. The Italian Federation of Mercer County to use auditorium October 19, November 9, January 11 for lecture course.

Societá Tammaro Femminile to use auditorium November 25 for entertainment.

December 3, 1936. The Italian-American Sportsmen's Club to use high school auditorium November 16, 17, 18, 19, 20 for entertainment.

July 1, 1937. Camera Dancing Studio to use Junior High School No. 4 auditorium for dance recital June 24.

January 6, 1938. Trenton Lodge Sons of Italy to use high school auditorium February 11 for entertainment.

February 3, 1938. *Societá Femminile Tammaro* to use high school auditorium January 26 for entertainment.

March 3, 1938. Venanzi Athletic Club to use Jefferson School gymnasium February 18 for games.

May 5, 1938. Italian Social Club to use high school auditorium April 28 for entertainment.

July 7, 1938. Florentine Studio of the Dance to use Junior High School No. 4 auditorium June 23 for dance recital.

November 3, 1938. Trenton Sons of Italy to use high school auditorium November 20 for presentation of play.

January 5, 1939. Ronzoni Program Company to use high school auditorium January 8 for entertainment.

February 2, 1939. *Societá Romana di M.S.* to use high school auditorium March 17 for entertainment.

March 2, 1939. Italian-American Civic League to use high school auditorium March 12 for entertainment.

April 6, 1939. *Societá Romana di M.S.* to use high school auditorium March 17 for entertainment.

The Italian-American Civic League to use high school auditorium April 16 for entertainment.

The Italian American Bocce Club to use high school auditorium May 6 for entertainment.

June 1, 1939. Italian American Group to use high school auditorium June 3 for entertainment.

September 7, 1939. Trenton Post No. 2 to use Robbins School auditorium September 22 for motion picture entertainment.

January 6, 1940. Daughters of Italy to use New Washington School auditorium May 27 for entertainment.

Italian American Bocce Club to use New Washington School auditorium June 1 for entertainment.

July 11, 1940. The Italian Social Club to use New Washington School auditorium June 22 for entertainment.

October 3, 1940. Italian Bocce Club to use Washington School auditorium September 28 for presentation of Italian play.

Italian American Club to use Washington School auditorium November 15 for entertainment.

November 7, 1940. Daughters of Italy to use high school auditorium November 15 for entertainment.

January 2, 1941. Radice Star Teams to use Grant School gymnasium Monday, December 20 for games.

February 6, 1941. *Societá Casteltermini Femminile* to use Grant School kindergarten third Tuesday of each month beginning February 18 for meetings.

Social Women's Club to use Washington School auditorium January 25 for Italian play.

Italian American Women's Welfare Committee to use high school auditorium March 7 for Italian play.

March 6, 1941. Italian Social Club to use Washington School auditorium February 22 for Italian play.

St. Gabriel Society to use high school auditorium April 19 for entertainment.

April 3, 1941. Villalba Society to use high school auditorium March 28 for entertainment.

Sons of Italy to use high school auditorium May 17 for entertainment.

October 9, 1941. Star of Italy to use high school auditorium October 25 for entertainment.

November 6, 1941. St. James R.C. Church to use Grant School auditorium for meeting and movie.

February 2, 1942. Committee of Loyal Americans of Italian Extraction to use high school auditorium February 28 for play, proceeds for American Red Cross War Relief Fund.

May 7, 1942. *Societá Femminile San Tammaro* to use Washington School auditorium May 2 for entertainment.

October 1, 1942. *Societá di M.S. Casteltermini* to use Grant School kindergarten for meetings September 20, October 20, November 17, December 15, January 19, February 6.

Loggia Adelaide Cairoli to use high school auditorium October 31 for entertainment.

Their Varied Activities

We have seen that as the number of Italian immigrants began to grow in Trenton in the 1880s and 1890s the need to organize became impelling and, one might say, imperative. The immigrant founders evidently thought of themselves in terms of their national origin when there were only a few from particular villages, towns or regions. We note, for instance, that the first three groups to be organized – in 1886, 1889, and 1892 – bore names that included terms such as Italian-American, Italo-American, and simply Italian.

It was not till 1894 that we find an association made up of men coming from a particular area: The Neapolitan Republican League. In 1896 the Roman Beneficial Society was organized. Among the first 10 groups to be organized we find that six were mutual aid societies, three were political organizations, and one listed its purposes as educational and patriotic. Of the six, two show area identification, which clearly marked many others that were to follow – *i.e.*, they were no longer Italian but Neapolitan, Roman, Sanfelese, for example.

We have also seen that the religious and spiritual needs of these immigrants had to be met. It is with the doings of the early church groups that we begin to find newspaper articles that first give us insight into the many and varied activities that those new Americans engaged in.

One reads, for example, that memorial services were held by the Italian Evangelical Congregation in the Chapel of the Calvary Baptist Church on September 2, 1900. About 100 persons attended and heard an address by the Rev. Vincent Serafini. During the services it was announced that a Garibaldi celebration was to be held in the same chapel on Thursday, September 20.[1] The article mentions that none of the Italian organizations was present. One wonders why they should absent themselves, since by 1900 nine organizations had incorporated. Surely members of these would also have been interested in memorial services for so widely admired and revered a national hero as Garibaldi; one can only speculate that perhaps the fact that the services were held by members of a Protestant church in the chapel of a Protestant church was the reason for their not attending.

Another meeting, held in Anchak's Hall at 841-843 South Broad Street on September 22, 1900, appeared as a news item. The purpose was to plan the construction of an Italian Catholic church. The article mentioned that the majority of the 4,000 Italians of the city would attend the Church of the Immaculate Conception, while the remainder were distributed among the various Catholic parishes of the city.[2]

We read that on September 23, 1900, the Rev. Luigi Pozzi told a crowd of nearly 500 Italians at Anchak's Hall that Bishop McFaul was in favor of the project to build a church. All present favored the erection of a church, and plans were made to collect subscriptions.[3] All, however, did not go smoothly. An article mentioned that factional disagreement broke out in the congregation of St. Joachim's Church because the Rev. A. Pozzi refused to allow the appointment of Prof. Vito Da Lorenzo as a trustee of the church; Father Pozzi had changed his mind and suggested Vito Lupo. Frank Lanza was selected to preside and P. Cella was named secretary. Other objectors stated that Father Pozzi had arranged matters to benefit himself. All present, however, agreed to send a telegram of condolence to Mrs. McKinley. The following day there was another notice stating that the Italians were still divided. The source of the fracas was felt to be factional: at odds were the Sanfelesi, with 1500 Sanfelesi as the most numerous in the city, the Romans with 1000, and last the Sicilians with no more than 15.[5] This last figure seems to be improbable.

There was, in spite of such factionalism, a happy ending to this enterprise. On July 16, 1904, the Italians celebrated the dedication of St. Joachim's Church. Father Aloysius Pozzi, the pastor, was credited with the successful erection of the church. Since the problem of language was a serious one, Father Pozzi translated Bishop McFaul's remarks into Italian. The affair was given color by the presence in full uniform of the Military Society of Bersaglieri,[6] who, before entering the church, had marched from their meeting place on Chestnut Avenue behind a band from Bristol, Pennsylvania. Because July 16 is also the feast day of Our Lady of Mount Carmel, the Bersaglieri held open house in the evening and there was a display of fireworks.[7]

At the turn of the century there were other activities that Trenton's early immigrant residents engaged in. On September 20, 1900, for example, a celebration was held by the Italians of Trenton and vicinity commemorating the anniversary of the taking of Rome by Giuseppe Garibaldi. This date, in Italy is frequently found as a street name – Via XX Settembre in Formia, for example. As was very common in Trenton at the time, there were both religious and secular services. However, because of the assassination of King Humbert of Italy on July 29, 1900, the Italians canceled their customary ceremony and picnic; religious services were held in the evening in the Chapel adjoining the Calvary Baptist Church with an address by the Rev. Vincent Serafini. The Garibaldi Society also met in commemoration that evening at their headquarters at 703 South Broad Street.[8]

It was in those days, too, that Trenton's Italians began to organize in political groups. A notice appeared announcing that on Monday, October 15, "Italians of this city" would meet "in the hall at 708 South Broad Street", when the Italian Republican Club was to be organized and officers elected. Plans were being made for parade.[9]

Other activities such as a ball held by the Metropolitan Band, under the leadership of Frank S. Lanza, took place.[10] On Wednesday, January 22, 1902, the thirteenth anniversary of the Washington and Victor Emanuel Society was celebrated in Columbus Hall, at 551 South Clinton Avenue. All families and friends of members enjoyed music, refreshments, and speeches.[11]

It was in those days, too, that we begin to find newspaper items describing the religious and street festivals that the Italians had brought with them to Trenton. In 1901 the Feast of Our Lady of Mount Carmel was celebrated. Ceremonies began early, at eight o'clock in the morning with the Bersaglieri, in full uniform, parading to the music of the Metropolitan Band, led by Frank S. Lanza. Solemn High Mass was celebrated in the Church of the Immaculate Conception by the Rev. Ignatius Berna; the sermon was delivered by the Rev. Aloysius Fish. In the evening, a splendid display of fireworks was seen by an estimated 2,000 spectators on the Roebling's lots on Swan Street. The Bersaglieri then served lunch [sic] in the parochial hall on Chestnut Avenue.[12]

In 1902 the Feast was held again. This was noted as a most elaborate ceremony at the Italian Catholic Church on Jennie Street, now Hudson Street, where the Rev. Father Pozzi officiated. Previous to the services there was a parade by the Second Italian Regiment of Bersaglieri, headed by Ruhlman's Band. Comment was made regarding the soldier's helmets and their irridescent greenish-blue cock's tail feathers. An outdoor celebration was held on the lots near South Broad and Jennie Streets, where a display of fireworks was shown. The committee in charge included Messrs. Faggella, Massari, Chianese, Carnevale, Buchicchio, and Gantiosa.[13]

By 1906 the Feast was said to have "a gorgeous service" following preparations made by the Bersaglieri Society.[14] In 1907 the "Italian Pageant", that is, the Feast of the Madonna SS. di Casandrino, was reported as having decorations of "unusual magnificence". Now it was held by members of "St. Joachim's Italian Church", and was said to be in the form of a carnival. On Saturday and Sunday 50 arches "constructed on Butler Street from South Clinton Avenue to Whittaker Avenue present a sight never before seen in the city. From these arches are suspended thousands of vari-colored glasses which will be illuminated". In front of the Church there was a stand made to accommodate two bands. The *Trenton Times* mentioned that the year before several thousand people had been attracted from all parts of the city.[15]

The early feasts achieved their striking illumination effects by the use of colored glass containers, like those that serve as votive lamps, in which were oil and a wick. One can imagine the work entailed in lighting all those lamps early in the evening. By 1920 the feasts had become more and more like those the Italians had celebrated in their home towns. The carnival atmosphere was created by the many stands put upon the sidewalks, at which one could buy filbert nuts shelled and strung on string, *torrone* (nougat candy with roasted almonds), *biscotti al anice* (anise flavored biscuits), *zeppole*, and clams on the half shell. Italian pastries were available at Landolfi's or Ciaramella's, both on Butler Street.

The solemn High Mass held at 11 o'clock on Sunday morning was highlighted by the *panegirico* (panegyric) delivered by a clergyman who had been invited from a church out of town. The panegyric, in praise of the revered Madonna SS. di Casandrino, was delivered in orotund tones and was extremely flowery in the Italian manner.

In the afternoon the procession was held. The school children, the women carrying candles, the men in their dark suits, the decorated float carrying the statue of *La Madonna*, and the usual two bands left the church and marched on Bayard, Butler, Elmer and Mott Streets. Many unaccustomed to the ways of the faithful were shocked to see that some of the viewers would approach the float and pin a one-dollar, two-dollar, or five-dollar bill to the gown of the Madonna.

In the evening the bands alternated in playing from the stands erected in front of the church. Fireworks were featured on Monday night to close the feast.

The feast that was held in 1921 was the prototype of all those that followed because it was the first to be illuminated by electricity. There were 6,000 electric bulbs of varied colors installed by Lawrence Soriero. Two bands played – the Cesare Battista and the Giuseppe Vezzella bands, both from Philadelphia. The panegyric was delivered by the Rev. Dr. Panbianco of Philadelphia and at five o'clock Sunday afternoon, groups marched in the procession. The two bands, in their evening concerts, vied for the $100 prize offered to the band acclaimed as rendering the better performance.[16]

In Italy great pride is taken in holding the annual saints' feast day celebrations, resulting, perhaps, in rivalry between or among the various parishes of the same town, or between those arranging for the feasts in neighboring towns. Our term parochialism in Italy is expressed by the phrase *spirito di campanilismo*, from the word *campanile* (bell tower), hence loyalty to one's church as symbolized by the bell tower. In my father's hometown of Formia, two feasts are held in the month of June – that of St. Erasmo on the second and that of St. John on the twenty-fourth. Each parish tries to outdo the other in the attractiveness of the street illumination, the length of its procession, the variety of its evening folklore parade, the quality of its bands, and the splendor of its fireworks display.

Among the Sicilians in North and East Trenton there were the feasts of St. Calogero, St. Joseph, and St. Anthony and in Chambersburg, as many as five feasts were held in the same year. John Conte, who came to Trenton on January 1, 1926 as an electrician, remembers working on the street illumination of the following feasts, all held in 1926: the Feast of St. Antimo in May, the Feast of St. Anthony in June, the Feast of Our Lady of Mount Carmel in July, the Feast of the Madonna of Casandrino in September, and the Feast of St. Vincent in October.

Church-related festivals were not the only activities that the Italians of Trenton engaged in; they also became actively involved in a number of causes, goals, and aspirations. Some, indeed, were achieved, such as the building of churches; others were delayed, and others simply died.

One early cause which came to naught at the time – it was not realized until 1959 – was the erection of a statue in honor of Christopher Columbus. With much interest manifested in such an undertaking, in September of 1911 a meeting was held in Eagle Hall, at 714 South Clinton Avenue. The movement initiated by two Italian sculptors, P. Guidotti and James Guidotti, greatly interested many residents in Chambersburg, who quickly stated their willingness to aid in the cause. The plans were to raise $25,000 to $40,000 for the "modelling" of the statue and for the purchase of a plot on which to place it.

This was not to be a purely Italian undertaking; it was to be multi-national, as was proper. Mayor Frederick W. Donnelly was named honorary president of the "international" committee in charge. Among the members of the committee were the following: D. Pierro, president; Di Leo, vice president; P. Di Leo, treasurer; M. Tarangelo, secretary. Others assisting in the project were Dr. R. Pantaleone, C.H. Micklin, Prof. De Lorenzo, A. Greenburg, Dr. J.M. Fuchs, L. Warady, and A. Elenevsky.[17]

Within six days there was further action. At a meeting held at 593 South Clinton Avenue, committees were appointed: Donato Pierro was named president; John P. Manze, vice president; Peter M. Dorsey, recording secretary; Gioacchino Guidotti, financial secretary; and James J.A. Tallone, treasurer.[18] Alas, nothing came of this; it would be years before further action was taken.

In the second and third decades of the twentieth century there were a number of causes which were hotly discussed among the Italians, some of whom became active supporters or adherents. One of those to become actively involved was Alfonso Bilancio. Recalling his work in the cause of woman's suffrage after he came here in 1910, he remembers that Carlo Marino translated articles on woman's suffrage written by a Mrs. McCormack. These were then published in pamphlet form by the five Bilancio brothers and distributed among interested persons in the Italian enclave.

He talks vividly, too, of their involvement in the demonstrations held when Carlo Tresca and Arturo Giovanitti were arrested as members of the I.W.W. (Industrial Workers of the World) and as conspirators. Carlo Tresca was described in the press as one of the most rapid leaders of industrial disturbance. In addition to voicing his political views, Mr. Giovanitti wrote powerful and touching poetry in English. Although information about these two men is rather scant, one article appearing on page 14 of the *New York Times* of October 1, 1917, sheds some light on their alleged activities. The article mentions that Tresca was the Italian leader of the I.W.W. (Industrial Workers of the World) and one of the "most rabid of the I.W.W. trouble-makers". The I.W.W., Tresca had recently said, was against all governments and advocated strikes. Giovanitti, another I.W.W. agitator, had been "prominent in the Paterson strike of 1913". Giovanitti, as the article noted, calls himself a "poet and a Socialist". Mr. Bilancio also recalls – as do many of us – the dark days of the Sacco-Vanzetti trial and execution. He spoke sadly of the meetings attended and the speeches heard in protest of what many felt to be grave injustice. Those interested may want to read a cogent article by the eminent lawyer and jurist, Felix Frankfurter, which appeared in the *Atlantic Monthly* of March 1927, pages 409-432. The article, entitled "The Case of Sacco and Vanzetti", presents the facts of the case, which had become a matter of international concern. Frankfurter writes of a "collusive effort between the District Attorney and agents of the Department of Justice" to rid the country of Sacco and Vanzetti because of their "Red activities". He states that "Judge Thayer's opinion confirmed old doubts" as to the guilt of the two Italians.

A project designed to benefit the general welfare of Trenton's Italians was undertaken in 1919. Because there had to be a concerted effort made by the Italian people in order to work toward so broad a purpose, it was decided to form a league. Representatives of nine organizations met on January 22, 1919, at 448 Whittaker Avenue and formed the Colonial League; its purpose was to assist Italians by encouraging attendance at evening schools and, in general, to improve the social welfare of the Italians. This group did not wish to be confused with the Italian Colonial Committee.[19]

The Italian Colonial Committee, however, did have a project that it sought to realize, best made clear by a letter from the Committee to the Trenton Board of Education.[20] The letter follows:

Italian Colonial Committee
Trenton, New Jersey
Richard D. La Guardia, Secretary

March 3, 1919

Mr. James S. Messler
President of the Board of Education
Trenton, New Jersey

Dear Sir:

As the Secretary of the Italian Colonial Committee of the City, I have been requested to write to you regarding the following matter: This committee has in mind the erection of a possible educational institution or a recreational centre of amusement for the Italians of this City.

For your information, if you do not know, the Italian Colonial Committee has organized originally and only for the up-liftment of the Italian people of this City for the sole purpose of betterment educationally and providing them with the proper entertainment. This will not only be of great advantage to the Italians but will mean an improvement of this city, itself. I know you are interested in both, and therefore, I am writing to you in this way.

The information I was required to ask was if the city is still willing to sell to them for this purpose the Centennial School building, which is situated on Butler and Whittaker, and if so, what is the best price the city will allow them for this purpose. I shall not attempt to give you the entire program of education and other features we are planning to carry out, but assure you that not one of them will be lacking in benefit and up-liftment. I will be glad to hear from you in this matter, and follow any suggestion you may have to give me.

May I call your attention to this Committee, and I would appreciate if you would make a note of it, as we are willing and anxious to cooperate with you in any program that may appear in which the Italians will be needed or wanted.

Thanking you for your kindness, I am,

Very cordially yours,

Richard D. La Guardia[21]

Again there was failure; nothing came of this offer to purchase the Centennial School. The idea, however, did not die: sixteen years later, in September of 1935, the Italian Federation of Mercer County made plans to hold a drive for the raising of $10,000 designated to be used for the construction of a community home, regarded as long needed by the 25,000 Italian American residents of Trenton and Mercer County.[22] This effort also proved to be fruitless.

In March of 1939 the idea was brought up again. This time the project was undertaken by a single organization, the *Societá Romana di M.S.*, which engaged Angelo Gloria and his company for entertainment to be given in the high school auditorium on Chambers Street. Proceeds from the affair would be added to the fund for the construction of a community center or social hall on the former site of the Centennial School,[23] where many of those active in this new undertaking had spent their elementary school years.

Plans were being implemented for the construction of a modern community home by the *Societá Romana di M.S.* on land the society had purchased from the Board of Education the former site of the Centennial School; the plot measured 100 by 200 feet. Construction, estimated to cost between $40,000 and $50,000, was scheduled to start in late summer with completion in January of the following year.[24]

On Sunday, October 8, 1939, the formal dedication of the Roman Hall and Recreation Center was held. The structure was blessed by the Rev. Alfred T. Sico, of St. Joachim's Church, at 1:30 p.m. This function was followed by a dinner. Gerald Perugini, vice president of the Roman Society, was the principal speaker; Dr. Albert F. Moriconi, chairman of the building committee, was the toastmaster. Musical entertainment followed, including vocal selections by Miss Josephine Salvatore and Miss Anne Giovanetti.[25]

When the Stock Market crashed in 1929, causing the Great Depression of the 1930s, Trenton's Italian Americans, along with millions of other Americans, felt the demoralizing effects of unemployment and the ravages of poverty. There were new and pressing matters to be addressed and solutions to be found. The Italian Welfare League was one group that set about providing aid for the needy; another was the Italian Business and Professional Men's Club, whose members, for example, planned to hold a dance in the Knights of Columbus Auditorium on December 17, 1930, the proceeds of which were to be given to the Italian Welfare League to distribute necessities to the Italian poor of the city.[26]

Some of Trenton's cultural activities and groups were also feeling the numbing pinch of lack of funds. One of these was the Trenton Symphony Orchestra, which benefited from the Seventh Annual La Nuova Capitale Picnic that was held on August 24, 1932; all the proceeds of the picnic were earmarked for the Trenton Symphony Orchestra. The picnic was held at the Italian-American Sportsmen's Club. Michael Commini was the general chairman, assisted by John Curry. The affair was awaited eagerly by the Italians because the Trenton Symphony Orchestra was announced as the main attraction. Soloists were Louise Masino of Trenton and Louis Mainiero of Bridgeport, Connecticut. Chairmen of the various committees were as follows: music, Robert Jannelli; publicity, Dr. Joseph Pantaleone; reception, the Hon. Daniel A. Spair; advisory, Miss Frances Francalangia and Miss Magna Kejval; bazaar, J. Paternoster; decoration, Albert Dal Corso; novelties, James P. Fry; moving pictures, Harry Episcopo; refreshments, Stephen Faggella; luncheon, Domenico Buchicchio; games, Carmelo Severino; tickets, Archesano Brillantini; parade, Armando Agabiti; transportation, E. Angelucci; grounds, Anthony Rebecca.[27]

In January of 1934 another attempt was made to organize the Italians of Mercer County. In union there was to be the strength needed to confront and cope with the problems of the day. On January 30, Dr. Joseph Pantaleone and Michael Commini outlined the project to a group that met in Nardi's Hall. A temporary committee named by Mr. Commini included Peter Di Antonio, Natale Masciantoni, George Calisti, Antonio Benedetti, Dr. Joseph Pantaleone, Ralph Di Donato, Dr.Anthony J. Lettiere, Samuel Naples, Joseph Plumeri, Vincenzo Giuliano, Samuel Caltagirone, Arthur Salvatore, John Boscarell, James Marolda, Amedeo Ciabattone, and Michael Commini.[28]

Further plans were made at a meeting held on February 9 in the Casteltermini Hall for a Federation of the Italian Societies of Mercer County whose purpose was to work for the betterment of the Italian citizens. Over 100 persons attended the session.[29]

Under the auspices of the Welfare Committee of the Italian Federation of Mercer County, the *Circolo Filodrammatico Coloniale* presented Shakespeare's *Othello* (or *Il Moro di Venezia*, the Moor of Venice in Italian) on May 24, 1935, in the Trenton Central High School Auditorium. This too was an attempt to raise money to help the needy.[30]

Another group organized in those difficult days was the Unity League. On May 30, 1935, permanent officers of the board of directors were elected at a meeting held in Commini's Restaurant. The officers were Charles Cella, president; James Fuccello, vice president; Frank Di Giuseppe, secretary; Henry Commini, treasurer; Peter Cantiosa, assistant secretary; Nicholas Dondiego, assistant treasurer; and Anthony Vitella, sergeant at arms. The board of directors consisted of Michael Commini, Victor Del Gaudio, Joseph Travis, Peter Peroni, and James Vitella. The group planned its first activity: a dance to be held June 4 at the Eldorado Hall.[31]

Early in 1936 the members of the Italian Federation of Mercer County planned to participate in the observance of Music Week. A committee to channel the efforts of the organization was headed by Michael Commini; he was assisted by Michael Volpe, Louis Mazarri, and Peter Radice. Joseph Pantaleone was president of the Federation.[32]

In February of 1936, at a regular luncheon meeting of the Unico Club held in the Stacy-Trent Hotel, Dr. Joseph Pantaleone reported progress on the work being done to prevent crime committed by youths. Trenton Unico Club members also paid tribute to Mario Volpe, a member of the organization, who had been admitted the day before to the practice of law in New Jersey. Joseph Plumeri presided.[33]

Interest in the prevention of crime by youths continued to be part of Trenton Unico's program of civic activites. In an address to the club at its January 1939 meeting by psychologist Dr. Joseph L. Todino, of Garfield, N.J., on the subject of juvenile delinquency, Dr. Todino pointed out that a coordinated community program would be necessary to stamp out the problem. Amerigo D'Agostino, president of the club, announced that the organization would shortly undertake a similar study in Trenton. Board of directors elected at the meeting were Mario H. Volpe, Samuel Colletti, Peter

Fabian, Joseph Guidotti, Angelo Lupo, Michael Lanzara, and Daniel Spair. Committees appointed included: membership, Erasmo Ciccolella; entertainment, Peter W. Radice; publicity, Michael Pagano; public affairs, Dr. Joseph Pantaleone; ways and means, Joseph Plumeri.[34]

The Italian Federation of Mercer County was actively engaged in another undertaking in June of 1936. Among the questions discussed at a meeting held June 1 at the International Institute was that of making available a community center for the activities of the WPA Leisure Time Division, which was planning recreational work to include the Chambersburg section.[35]

The year 1936 also saw two especially interesting observances of Columbus Day. The rather elaborate nature of these observances may be explained perhaps by the fact that the year 1936 marked the 430th anniversary of the death of Columbus in 1506. One, held under the auspices of the Italian Federation of Mercer County in the Casteltermini Hall, with Mario H. Volpe presiding, featured an address in English by Peter T. Campon of Binghamton, N.Y., and an address in Italian by Dr. Domenico Vittorini, member of the Department of Foreign Languages at the University of Pennsylvania. Sub-committees for the affair were headed by Louis Mazarri, entertainment; Salvatore Marinari, program; Dr. James A. Durso, hall; and Peter W. Radice, publicity.[36]

The other observance of Columbus Day was on a much larger scale. For the program, to be held on Saturday, October 11, in the auditorium of the Trenton Central High School at 2:30 p.m., local parishes were organizing their children for choral singing, and the Independent Order Sons of Italy were to march into the auditorium in a body.[37] According to the newspaper account, more than 2,000 attended the tribute to Columbus.[38]

Another undertaking by an Italian group was that of the Italian American Republican League of Mercer County's canvass of Italian voters throughout Mercer County. The goal of this project was to seek an answer to the higher-than-usual plaint for more jobs in 1936. This was a move to produce more public jobs — i.e., the group was working toward getting greater recognition of Italians for political appointments.[39]

Italian groups were responding to cries for help. In 1937 the Italian-American Sportsmen's Club planned to hold a spaghetti dinner at the clubhouse on Kuser Road, the proceeds of which would be turned over to the Red Cross, which was raising funds for the victims of floods. Joseph Mainiero was chairman of the committee in charge, with Armando Agabiti as treasurer and Lino Fiorelli as secretary.[40]

Columbus Day in 1937 was celebrated by a commemoration of the 445th anniversary of the discovery of America, held on Sunday, October 17, at 7:30 p.m. in the Villalba Hall, at 31 George Street. The committee for the celebration consisted of Cataldo Valenti, president; Frank La Paglia, secretary; Carmelo Guagliardo, treasurer; Giuseppe Mulé, Michele Novembre, Vincent Fiorello, Vincent Bonfante, Joseph Plumeri, Onofrio Calderone, Raffaele Nalbone, Albert Di Maria, Quintilio Casciani, Antonio Cammarata, and Domenic Gambino.[41]

The renovating fund of the Immanuel Presbyterian Church, located at Whittaker and Roebling Avenues, was substantially increased from the proceeds of a concert presented on December 1, 1938, by the American Legion Glee Club at the church. The committee for the affair consisted of Sam Pagliaro, chairman; Nickolas De Angelo, tickets; Joseph Petta, publicity; and Albert Greco, chairman of the church's Christian Endeavor Society. Also lending a hand was the Rev. Michael P. Testa, pastor of the church.[42]

Involvement in community problems was highlighted at the anniversary meeting of the Italian-American Civic League held at the Trenton Central High School in March of 1939 when the Rev. Joseph Bolognese spoke of the League's activities: endorsement of the Trenton housing program; of the Trenton Committee on Municipal Recreation; of the appeal of the Committee of Electric Consumers for an investigation of rates; and condemnation of the failure of Mercer County Asemblymen to support Bill No. 453. The Welfare Committee, headed by Gennaro Cardelia, launched a summer camp program for underprivileged children of Italian origin. The Americanization Committee, chaired by Francis A. Caputo, was supporting legislation favoring the reduction of fees in the process of Americanization. On Sunday, April 16, the League was to present a play in the Central High School Auditorium, the proceeds of which were to go to the Bay Point Summer Camp for Children, located at West Point Pleasant.[43]

Other organizations responded to the call for assistance issued by the Italian-American Civic League. A novelty party, for example, under the auspices of the Trenton Italian Business and Professional Men's Club, held the evening of January 25, 1940, at the Roman Hall raised money to be given to the Civic League to be used to send underprivileged Italian children to summer camp.[44]

The Italian-American Civic League continued to broaden its concerns and activities. Robert V. Janelli, Trenton musician and president of the League, stated that "the League is about to sponsor a program of Family service for Italians in cases where a language handicap is involved".[45]

In March of 1940 the Italian Social Service Centre opened at 232 Hamilton Avenue, sponsored and financed by the Italian-American Civic League. It was designed to carry on professionlly all the phases of social work for needy Italians and Italian Americans. Miss Sylvia Manzi, executive secretary of the centre, supervised all activities. She was assisted by Mrs. Joseph Bolognese, social investigator; by Mrs. Inez Libori Jones, and by Miss Anette Di Gianni.[46]

In another effort to help the League, members of the "Italian Community

Day" Committee met in June of 1940 in the Roman Hall to hear a report from Angelo Salerno. An outing was planned, the proceeds of which would revert to the Italian-American Civic League to send 100 underprivileged children to summer camp at Browns Mills. The general chairman was Carl Maiorino. Daniel Brenna was in charge of the popularity contest committee.[47]

On Sunday, August 11, 1940, the Unity League had a family outing at the Italian-American Sportsmen's Club. A softball game between married men and members of the Ladies' Auxiliary, quoits, running races, a singing and dancing contest, and other activities were part of the program. Chicken *alla cacciatora*, corn on the cob, minestrone, and spaghetti were served.[48]

On September 21, 1940, the Italian-American Civic League opened its second annual drive for funds to make possible the continuance of family and social service work. In the past six months the Social Service Centre had assisted Italian-Americans with citizenship, registrations, relief, private employment, pensions, compensation, medical treatment, maternal aid, and general social service. Summer health-care for underprivileged children was an important program sponsored by the League. Carl J. Maiorino was general chairman of the drive.[49]

On Wednesday, February 5, 1941, a novelty party, chaired by Mrs. Agnes C. Kollatsch, was held under the auspices of the Italian-American Women's Welfare Committee at the Roman Hall at 8 p.m. This was the first of a series of programs benefiting the Italian-American Civic League, Inc. for the year 1941. Planned for March 7 was a benefit drama, *La Vergine della Foresta* (The Virgin of the Forest), to be given in the Trenton Central High School Auditorium.[50]

Easter of 1941 was more pleasant than it might have been for 50 indigent families of North Trenton, South Trenton, East Trenton, and Chambersburg because of baskets of food distributed by the Welfare Committee of the Italian-American Civic League, in cooperation with the Nicastro Distributing Co. of Trenton.[51]

At a meeting of the Italian-American Civic League held at the Casteltermini Hall, Gennaro Cardelia Sr., chairman of the Welfare Committee, reported that in January, February, and March, 108 clients were served by the League. Attorney Michael Felcone, chairman of the summer camp committee, reported that Grand Venerable Angelo Ruffo of the Independent Order Sons of Italy, a pioneer worker and organizer of mutual aid and benefit societies within the State of New Jersey, promised to have all his affiliate societies in the Trenton area participate in the summer camp work in 1941.[52]

To show what it was accomplishing, the Italian-American Civic League gave a presentation of its summer camp activities at a meeting of the Giovanni Bovio Mutual Aid Benefit Society held at the Casteltermini Hall on Sunday, April 27, 1941, at 2:30 p.m.[53]

In 1941 the Trenton Unico Club was among the organizations sponsoring the "I Am an American" program at Cadwalader Park on Sunday, May 18 at 3 p.m.[54]

The grounds of St. James R.C. Church were open for a nine-day benefit carnival and bazaar. Riding and other amusement devices were featured. Proceeds went to the defraying of expenses for repairs on the church property.[55]

In June of 1941 the Italian-American Civic League became the Columbus Civic League. It held its second Community Day Festival.[56]

Among the organizations pledging support to the fourth annual camp program of the Columbus Civic League was the Trenton Unico Club. Other organizations contributing to the League's Fund were the Grand Council of the Independent Order Sons of Italy and the Chambersburg Business and Professional Women.[57]

In September of 1941 the Community Chest recognized the Columbus Civic League by making it a member of its Council of Social Agencies.[58]

In 1942 the Columbus Social Service Centre had a full-time social worker: Miss Lieta Marchesi.[59]

Italian fraternal organizations in 1942 made elaborate preparations for the upcoming Labor Day Parade. A mass meeting was held at the Roman Hall for all of the officials.[60]

Americanization

In the early years of this century much was made of the terms "the melting pot" and Americanization. The concept of the melting pot was that the various ethnic strains should somehow fuse together into an alloy or amalgam which would then be a composite that could be called American. To bring this about it was necessary that the common language of this country – English – become the language of the new man, the amalgam to be created. It was also necessary that this new man, by a process of gentle inculcation, acquire the basics of Americanism. In the last century the process of naturalization did not cause any concern because the number of immigrants was not yet great, but with the great waves of Americans to be coming from the 1880s to the 1920s, the problem became serious enough to demand community attention.

The minutes of the Trenton Board of Education throw some light on what the Trenton school system, an arm of the city government, was doing to cope with the problem.

The minutes of the Board for December 2, 1909, contain a report of the Committee on Evening Schools stating that evening schools were opened for the Poles of the city. The report goes on to say that the committee engaged the services of the Rev. Aloys Fish, Ph.D., for the fee of $50 to give a course of lectures on United States history and civics in the Italian language, Tuesday and Thursday evenings, beginning November 30th. The committee also arranged for the advertisement of the classes by handbills in the Polish and Italian languages.

By 1914 we begin to find newspaper accounts of efforts made to bring to the immigrants opportunities to learn English and by so doing have an easier time in becoming an integral part of a non-Italian-speaking community. In 1914, for example, Miss Amandine Micoll, who was in charge of the kindergarten attached to the Italian Evangelical Congregation on Whittaker Avenue, of which the Rev. Vincent Serafini was the head, organized a class for the teaching of English to Italian women. Classes were held Tuesday, Wednesday, and Friday evenings each week. She already had a class of Italian women who met Tuesday afternoons from 3 to 4:30 o'clock. The Rev. Serafini was teaching English to young Italian men and boys.[1]

The minutes of the Board for the October 3, 1918, meeting show that the Committee on Evening Schools recommended that: 1) a class in English for foreign-speaking women be organized at the International Institute and that Miss Elizabeth Maloney be assigned as teacher; 2) classes in English for foreign-speaking men be organized at the plant of the American Steel and Wire Company, and that Mr. H.D. Marts be assigned as teacher.

That these decisions by the Board were of concern to the Italians is clear. The International Institute, situated at South Clinton Avenue and Beatty Street, was conveniently accessible to the Hungarians of that area and to the Italians of Chambersburg.

In 1919 the minutes of the Board for January 2 show that the range of activity was being enlarged. The Committee recommended that the organization of a class in English for foreigners at the Thomas Maddock Sons Company be approved and that Mr. Joseph Hoffman be appointed evening school teacher in charge of the class at a salary of "$2.50 per night". On November 6, 1919, the committee submitted further recommendations: that classes be formed at St. Joachim's Parochial School and that teachers be assigned as follows – foreigners, Miss Helen Swem; commercial work, Miss Miriam Lernered. It was understood that the stenography manuals and the typewriters would be furnished by the parochial school authorities.

From this it would seem that there were also attempts made to offer vocational training. Further growth can be seen taking place in the school system's program; for instance, the minutes for October 6, 1921, show that provision was made for a teacher of "a foreign class" at the American Steel and Wire Company, the Washington School, the McClellan School, the International Institute, and Junior High School No. 1 – all in areas where there were many Italians.

The minutes for November 1, 1923, recorded that classes were formed for the "non-English" at Junior High School No. 1, Franklin School, McClellan School, and the International Institute.

In 1928 the minutes for November 1 show that the International Institute of the Y.W.C.A. was adding another dimension to the School Board's program. It requested the free use of a room in the McClellan School on Tuesday afternoons and evenings for the purpose of social and educational clubs for Italian girls and women.

The minutes for March 5, 1931, record the enrollment in the evening school classes of the Foreign-Born Residents Citizenship Schools:

School	No. of Pupils	No. of Teachers
Junior High School No. 1	38	2
Junior High School No. 4	64	3
Skelton School	42	2
McClellan School	19	1
Washington School	80	3

It should be noted that all the schools listed, with the exception of the Washington School, offered vocational courses; at the Washington School teaching was limited to the English language and citizenship. Most of those attending the Washington School evening classes were from the Italian enclave in Chambersburg.

That Italians were making efforts to be naturalized can be seen from an article appearing under the headline "New Citizens Can Vote Nov. 8". Among the 250 new citizens were the following: Luigi Tritta, Michael Paternoster, Pietro Sprattoni, Ugo Aprile, Alfonso Verzilli, Daniel Brienzo, Gabriel Angelini, Niose Cappelletti, Nicola Bartolino, Gennaro Rizziello, Battista Fruscione, Matteo Di Nola, Salvatore Piazza, Mauro Corrente, Ottavio Vannozzi, Giuseppe Gibilisco, Filippo Lucidi, Giovanni Marino, Pietro Benedetti, Domenico Migliaccio, Francesco Capasso, Antonio Coppola, Vincenzo Sciarrotta, Vincenzo De Santis, Virgilio Mattia, Filippo Marchetti.[2]

The Salvatore Piazza mentioned above is the same Salvatore Piazza who graciously consented to be interviewed.

The teaching of English and the training for citizenship were now combined. In 1936, for example, the International Institute ran notice that beginning in mid-January, classes in English and citizenship would be held at the International Institute Tuesday, Wednesday, Thursday, and Friday evenings from 7 to 8 o'clock.[3] From the two teachers appointed – Miss Linda Alvino and Miss Anna Hudapka – we may infer that now an effort was being made to get teachers who could best cope with the language problems that were sure to be encountered.

By the late 1930s the work of citizenship had been taken up by the newly founded Italian-American Civic League. It formed the Americanization Committee, naming its chairman Francis A. Caputo. This group picked April, 1939, as "Americanization Month" to promote citizenship as strongly as possible. Mr. Caputo, for example, attended the third annual convention of the Italian Committee Immigrant Welfare Group in New York City.[4]

The Community Welfare Drive run by the Italian-American Civic League raised funds for its social service through its Social Service Center, some of whose efforts were directed to the acquiring of citizenship. Delegates were chosen in 1941 to attend the fifth annual conference of the American Committee for the Protection of the Foreign Born. The Civic League Americanization Committee made plans to initiate classes in citizenship for residents of North and East Trenton. These classes were held at the St. James School for both beginners and advanced pupils. The committee took advantage of visual aids in its classes. Films were shown about such topics as Washington, shrines of American patriotism, the story of our flag.[5]

At the League's November meeting held in the Casteltermini Hall, films were shown on the Declaration of Independence, the Constitution, and the National Government for the members of the League's Americanization and Citizenship classes.[6]

In 1942, beginners and advanced classes in citizenship were shown a "talkie" movie depicting the highlights of early America and present-day government at the Columbus Social Service Centre.[7]

In November of 1942 classes in Americanization, citizenship, and literacy, promoted at the St. James School by the Columbus Civic League in cooperation with the War Services Education Bureau of the WPA, received the grateful approval of the community. The classes that evening were shown films from the New Jersey State Museum on American History and present-day government. Casper Fantauzzo was in charge of the film projection.[8]

In Political Activities

Italian immigrants banded together in organizations, as we have said, largely because in organized groups they could provide aid for members in time of need. They soon saw that they should organize for another reason — politics. It comes as no surprise, then, that, after two mutual aid societies had been founded in 1886 and in 1889, the third organization to be founded was the Italian Republican Club of Trenton, N.J., incorporated in 1893. Just four months later, in March of 1894, the second political club, the Neapolitan Republican League, was founded.

Some individuals had been taking an active role in politics in peripheral ways. Vito Dileo, for example, as foreman of the yard gang at the Roebling's plant on South Clinton Avenue regularly got his charges out on election day to vote the Republican ticket.

In 1899 the Italian Democratic Club of Trenton, N.J., was incorporated. From this time on we find that the number of Italian political clubs continued to grow.

What follows will show that Italian Americans were slowly beginning to appear in the political life of Trenton and of Mercer County.

By 1915 the name of Anthony Spair appeared on the ballot as a Socialist favoring a small Board of Freeholders.[1] Three days later, in a box in the *Daily State Gazette* under the headline "How Freeholder Board Will Stand", there appeared the name of Michael Commini for the Ninth Ward. He was the first Italian American to hold an elective office.[2]

In 1919, Daniel A. Spair, Trenton lawyer, was appointed secretary of the Mercer County Board of Taxation.[3]

At a meeting of the Italian-American State Executive Republican Committee, the Rev. Vincent Serafini was elected president and Daniel A. Spair was elected secretary. The purpose of the association was to promote the Americanizing of more Italians and to further the campaign of Newton A.K. Bugbee for governor.[4]

In 1923 Michael Commini ran a paid political advertisement as a candidate for the City Commission.[5] The local Italian press ran a front page devoted to candidates for the city commission that year, two of the candidates being Michael Commini and Frank S. Lanza.[6]

In the same year Frank Muccioli, who had been serving as acting clerk of the City District Court, was appointed to the clerkship by Judge Charles A. English. Muccioli had taken civil service examinations and had passed with the high average of 86.50. He was, according to the article, a former service man and had attended the evening high school and Rider College.[7]

In 1926 a newspaper item carried the information that Michael Commini, who had been naturalization clerk at the Mercer County Court House for the past nine years, would end his service in that capacity and go into private business.[8]

In 1927 Daniel A. Spair was being boomed as a candidate for one of the three Representative Assembly nominations from Mercer County.[9]

Italian American activity, of course, was not limited to running for political office. Organizations sponsored affairs for elected officials. In 1927, for example, members of the Circolo Italiano unanimously endorsed the then City Commission at a testimonial dinner held in their clubhouse on Hamilton Avenue.[10]

Italian American Republicans from Trenton and vicinity held a rally in the Trenton High School Auditorium at 8 p.m. on June 14, 1930 in the interest of Dwight W. Morrow's candidacy for the United States Senate on the Republican ticket. Among the speakers were Attilio Giannini, international banker; and John M. Di Silvestro, banking official of Philadelphia. Chairman C. Thomas Chianese planned a program of music furnished by Napoliello's band.[11]

In 1936 Michael A. Pagano was elected president of the new Italian-American Young Republican Club, which was organized January 5 in Nardi's Hall.[12]

Also in 1936 Arthur A. Salvatore was named chairman of the board of governors of the Young Democrats of Mercer County at the meeting held in Democratic Headquarters on East State Street.[13]

Some of the political clubs also served a social purpose. The Italian-American Young Republicans of Mercer County, for example, planned a dance to be held May 15, 1936.[14]

The Chambersburg Republican Club held a spaghetti supper as a feature of its meeting on May 12, 1936.[15]

Lest we think that there were only Republicans or Democrats among the Italian Americans, there were also Independents. The Italian-American Independent Club of North Trenton held an outing at Eggerts Crossing on June 28, 1936. Alex Farina was the general chairman, assisted by Patsy Caserta.[16]

Joseph Plumeri was elected for the fourth time as president of the North Trenton Republican Club. Others elected were Vincenzo Fiorello, vice president; Rosalino Guarino, secretary; Vincenzo Cacciatore, financial secretary; Paul J. Plumeri, treasurer; and Giuseppe Corallo, sergeant at arms. Members of the Board of Directors were Giovanni Nalbone, Francesco Butera, Giuseppe Piazza, Michele Fruscione, and Michele Lombardo.[17]

The first meeting of the Seventh Ward Democratic Club was held on February 23, 1937, at the home of James Eppolito, 437 Princeton Avenue. The officers elected were James Eppolito, president; Joseph Zaccone, vice president; Louis Di Francisco, second vice president; Vincent R. Panaro, recording secretary; and Joseph Lutterio, treasurer.[18]

One cannot miss the political overtones in the testimonial dinner held in honor of Governor Harold G. Hoffman by the Italian-American Sportsmen's Club in its clubhouse. Joseph Felcone, toastmaster, presented the governor with a life membership. About 500 persons were in attendance.[19]

In 1938 Miss Marie Maiorino was a member of the committee arranging for the spaghetti supper to be served by the Ladies' division of the Crawford Jamieson Booster Club.[20]

Another special occasion, attended by more than 900 persons, was the testimonial dinner held in the Stacy-Trent Hotel in honor of George Pellettieri, who had recently been appointed judge of the City District Court. The affair was sponsored by the Italian American organizations.

Addresses were delivered in English and Italian. Speakers included Senator Crawford Jamieson; Felix Forlenza, assistant prosecutor of Essex County; Dr. Vincenzo Di Virgilio, president of Philadelphia's Abruzzi Unione; Angelo Ruffo, Grand Venerable of the Independent Order Sons of Italy; Frank S. Katzenbach, 3rd, who represented Governor Moore; and J. Albert Homan. A musical program followed. A special feature was the appearance of Miss Rose Marie, radio star, who sang several selections. Michael Commini was general chairman.[21]

On Sunday, April 28, 1940, the members of the Italian-American Sportsmen's Club held a testimonial dinner in honor of Assemblyman Mario H. Volpe, in their auditorium on Kuser Road. Michael Commini was chairman of the committee, assisted by Alphonse Pone, secretary; Prosecutor Andrew J. Duch, treasurer; and Rocco F. Pagano, director of publicity.[22]

In 1942 in the Republican contests for positions on the ballot Peter S. Racine drew the number one spot in the fourth district of the Ninth Ward for the Republican County Committee. In the only other Republican Committee contest Michael Capiello was first, with Frank R. Vitella second for the second district of the tenth ward.[23]

Education: One of Their Concerns

The first Italian American to graduate from Trenton High School was Nicholas Americus Camera in the class of 1900. His sister Mary, of the class of 1901, was the second to be graduated. Since these were children born here in Trenton to Angelo and Maddalena Camera, we know that there were children of Italian American parents in the elementary schools as early as 1882 and undoubtedly even earlier.

Italian Americans were indeed sending their children to the public schools. Many of these children entered the schools with no knowledge of the English language, as was the case with my brother Angelo, my sister Olga, and me along with many of our neighbors' children. Italian was the language spoken at home; it would be more accurate to say that a dialect was spoken at home – ours was Neapolitan. One can well imagine what a serious problem this was for both pupils and teachers. To cope with this the Board of Education made an attempt at providing a solution. The Minutes of the Board for the July 2, 1908, meeting record that "a special class be organized in the Hewitt School for Italian children who do not speak English and that Miss Alice Camera be assigned as teacher of that class under appointment to be dated September 14th, 1908". Alice was the sister of Mary, who had been hired in 1904, and of Florence, who was hired in 1914.

As young Italian Americans were being graduated from Trenton High School and from the Normal School, they were being hired by the Trenton school system, perhaps because they not only met all qualifications but they also were assumed to understand and speak Italian.

Meanwhile St. Joachim's Church had bought land and raised funds for an elementary school, which was opened in 1910. The St. James School was opened in 1923. Both schools were staffed by nuns of the Italian teaching order Le Maestre Pie Filippini.

As was learned from a minutes book found among the records of St. Joachim's Church, a problem arose in 1919. The minutes were kept in Italian, and on a label attached to the cover was written "Committee Pro Italian School". This struck me as odd, because there had been an Italian school in operation at St. Joachim's since 1910. Why another school? The minutes revealed that there was a problem and that there were, in fact, several reasons for it.

In 1912 the Rev. Edward Griffin had replaced the Rev. Pozzi, founder and first pastor of St. Joachim's Church. One assumes that Father Griffin, recognizing the realities of financing a school, had broached the idea of turning over the school to the public school system of Trenton. This was perhaps the major cause for a number of the male parishioners to form a committee on January 16, 1919. The committee listed three complaints (here I translate): 1) that in 1912 the rector of the Italian St. Joachim's Church aimed to rent the parish school to the city of Trenton for public instruction to the detriment of the Italian language and of the Catholic education of the student body; 2) that without the knowledge of the Filippini Sisters, teachers in the said parochial school, he had taken for St. Joachim's Church the house at 27 Bayard Street, acquired by the said nuns at great sacrifice and privation to themselves; 3) that the said rector aimed to use American nuns for instructional purposes with the probable discharging of the Italian Sisters with the pretext of eliminating parish expenses. Considering these complaints, the committee deliberated as follows:

a. to unite all Italian Catholics and fervent supporters of the Italian school;

b. to elect a president, a secretary, a reliable treasurer, and two trustees;

c. to nominate a committee of many members to gather signatures and money to reduce the debt of the school, so that these may be given to his Excellency the Bishop of Trenton, and to apply for an Italian pastor, able and energetic, and that the continuance of Italianism in the church and in the school be guaranteed;

d. Should an Italian pastor not be provided, the donors will receive the amounts donated. Also anyone may dispose of such sums as he wishes for the sisters or the church.

e. Gifts are not to be less than $5.00.

This was decided on February 2, 1919, at 113 Bayard Street. The group named itself The Committee Pro the Italian School. Dr. G. Tempesto was elected president; Domenico Buchicchio, vice president; Antonio Bella, secretary; Antonio Vella, assistant secretary; and Umberto Salamandra, treasurer.

A Collection Committee was formed and divided into sections. Section 1 consisted of Raffaele Gervasio, Antonio Vella, and Giovanni D'Abbronzo. They were to canvass residents on Hamilton Avenue, Bayard Street, Butler Street, and Clark Street from Canal Street to Chestnut Avenue.

Section 2 consisted of Mattia Di Mattia, Nicola Guida, Gennaro Cardelia, Antonio Ghiottone, and Tommaso Mirando. They were assigned to Clinton Avenue to Mott Street, including New Street.

Section 3 consisted of Felice Nardi, Salvatore Valeriani, and Umberto Salamandra. These were to go from Clinton Avenue to Chestnut Avenue on Swan Street, Roebling Avenue, Emory Avenue, Morris Avenue, and Fulton Street.

Section 4 consisted of Francesco Di Marco, Romolo Venanzi, Ascensio Angelini, and Felice Marchetti. They were to go from Chestnut Avenue to Anderson Street; Hamilton Avenue to Morris Avenue, on Roebling Avenue, College Street, and Kent Street.

Section 5 consisted of Michele Del Prete, Giuseppe Perferi, Pasquale Arbitelli, Antonio Peroni, and Domenico Cristoforo. These were to canvass Washington Street and Franklin Street from Hamilton Avenue to Liberty Street.

On February 16, 1919, a meeting was held in the Savoia Hall on Clinton Avenue, at which time the sections turned in $467.75, which was deposited in the Mercer Trust in the name of the *Organizzazione Coloniale Italiana — Pro Scuola Italiana.*

It was decided that a committee, consisting of Domenico De Angelis and Giovanni Massari, was to collect from local businessmen. Raffaele Gervasio, Antonio Vella, and Giovanni D'Abbronzo were appointed to collect in Bordentown. Others were asked to collect from Brunswick Avenue to Hamilton Avenue, starting at Perry Street; others were to solicit funds in South Trenton.

By March 2, 1919, $1178.17 had been collected. Further collections showed the following amounts: by March 9, $1320.92; March 16, $1767.42; April 6, $2204.75; and June 1, $2652.75.

Their efforts had succeeded; their fears had been put to rest. The Filippini Sisters are still part of the teaching staff. Father Griffin was transferred in 1919 and replaced by Father Michael Di Ielsi, who after one year was replaced by the Rev. Alfonso Palombi.

Some four years later, on June 3, 1923, there was a formal dedication in honor of Margaret, deceased wife of Martin A. Maloney, whose generosity provided funds for the erection of the St. James School. The teachers were also of the Filippini teaching order.

Five years before St. Joachim's was to open its elementary school, an article appeared in the local press concerning the novitiate vow and the celebration of the feast day of the Assumption on August 15. At the High Mass celebrated by the Rev. Father Targia in St. Joachim's Church, the sermon was preached by Father Pozzi. It is noteworthy because he urged his congregation to help themselves to rise to a higher station in life. He also urged them to look to the education of their children. He said that they should not let their children become bootblacks, but should send their children to school so that they might strive for higher things, for the professions.[1]

In the second decade of this century Italian parents were proud to see their children's names in the newspaper for having been named to the Honor Roll or for having had an excellent attendance record. At the Columbus School, for example, a third grader whose name was listed in the Honor Roll was Angelo Terrava. Second graders were Anna Capizzi, Jennie Corroda, Angelo Scotto, John Matiste, and Bertha Zoda. First graders were Christopher Terrava, Pepino Immordaio, Joseph Spranza, Mary Zoda, Tony Terrava, Angelina Scotto, and Anna Rebecca.[2]

Among Trenton High School students on the Honor Roll in 1919 was Michael Felcone, of class A 3.[3]

On the Franklin School's attendance rolls, the following were neither absent nor tardy in December: in eighth grade A – Marion Rita; in eighth grade B – Marie Lettiere; in eighth grade C – Frank Acolia; in seventh grade A – Anthony Bilella; in seventh grade B – John Pongo; in sixth grade B – Joseph Acolia; in second grade C – Elvo Carocci, Elmo Carocci, and John Luisi; in first grade B – Raphael Di Naples.

The Honor Roll at the Monument School carried the names of Maria Perillo in fourth grade and of Saturday Rubino in third grade.[4]

Michael Felcone, member of the Junior Class at Trenton High School, placed second with an average of 89.52 on the Honor Roll.[5] He continued to appear on the Honor Roll in his senior year.[6]

In 1920 honor students at the Washington School included, in the sixth grade: Florence Brandi, Christina Trovannetti, Frank Gialella; in the fifth grade: Mary Graziano, Beatrice Loiocomo, Millie Pagliaro, Frank Basile; in the fourth grade: Lucy Zarilla, Daniel Brenna, Angelina Petrino, America Cantia, Angelo Bartolomei, Tony Marti; in the third grade: John Graziano, Tony Rachittoni, Anna Petruccio, Josephine Formicola, Frank Loucanno, and Florence Gambi.

The same issue carried the Centennial School Honor Roll for March. It included in the sixth grade: Mary De Angelo, Minnie Graziano, Chester Chianese, James Ferraro, Myrtle Graziano, Mary Pittaro, Anthony Chianese, John De Angelo, James Maida, and John Tancreda; in the fifth grade: Helen Rimo, Raphael Pettito; in the fourth grade: Mary Persico, Joseph Bonfield, Pasquale Varchetto, Denise Tanzone, Lucy Carlucci, Pasquale Turano, Joseph Frascella, and Michael Salamandra; in the third grade: Fannie Felcone, Margaret Greco, Samuel Dileo, Lindo Alvino, Rose Poveromo, Fanny Delarossa, Margaret Pettito, Nancy Tanzone, Ideale Martone, Pasquale Petrino, Elizabeth Varchetto, Lena Maisto, and Joseph De Puglio.[7]

In 1929 an item headlined "High School Test Results Revealed" dealt with the test results of students in the commercial department at Trenton Senior High School who had taken tests to determine the high school's representatives in the district contest to be held at Highland Park. Among the top five in the rapid calculation contest was Rose Marangelo; in the shorthand contest among the top five was Mary Carozza.[8]

Italian Americans were among those who won awards in June of 1930 at the Trenton School of Industrial Arts, situated at the corner of West State and Willow Streets. The diplomas and awards were given in the ballroom of the Stacy-Trent Hotel. Among those sharing the Tantum Bequest was Arthur J. Maglia. The Connor Millwork Company award for architectural drawing went to, among others, Angelo Joseph Ferrara.[9]

Boys of the Trenton Senior High School Class of 1930 were guests of the Kiwanis Club at a dinner meeting held at the Hotel Hildebrecht. One of the awards of attendance prizes went to Walter Criscola. Two certificates of merit were awarded, one for the highest average of efficiency to William Capanello and one for the greatest improvement to Stephen Di Angelo.[10]

Also in 1930 we find Italian Americans among the graduates of the Evening High School. Constantine Donato, class president, completed his entire high school education in the evening classes. Another to do so was Catherine A. Rizziello. Other Italian American graduates that year were Fannie V. Greco, Charles J. Romeo, and Reynold A. Salvatore.[11]

The graduating class at the Immaculate Conception High School in 1930 gathered for their commencement exercises in the grammar school auditorium. Among the 44 graduates were Natalie Helen Bella, Constance Natalie Arcioni, Rose Frances Filipponi, Helen Jachette, Frances Miele, Firmina Cecilia Valeriani, Ida Angeline Venanzi, Rose Viola Zazzo, Wilton Francis De Marco, Oilando Joseph Perferi, John Roland Pinelli, and Joseph John Salvatore.[12]

Italian American organizations were making awards to boys and girls of Italian extraction to encourage students to finish their high school education and to strive for high achievement. The Trenton Italian Business and Professional Men's Club, for example, entertained 40 boys of the graduating classes of the high schools of the city at a luncheon in the Hotel Stacy-Trent. All the guests received "handsome" pocketbooks, and special awards were made to a number who had distinguished themselves along various lines. Those cited for special service or achievement included Mario Volpe, Leonard Mancuso, Walter S. Criscuolo, Rocco Acquaviva, James Apoldite, Stephen De Angelo, and William Cappiello.[13]

Classes in English for French-, German-, and Italian-speaking adults were given in the International Institute. Frank Caputo continued with his last term's class in Italian and a new class in Italian for beginners.[14]

In 1935 the first Dr. William J. Bickett Scholarship established by the Trenton Teachers' Association in memory of Dr. Bickett, deceased Superintendent of the Trenton Public Schools, was awarded. The recipient was Joseph A. Palermo.[15]

At this time the Unico Club made an award of a book to an Italian American student. The person chosen to make the presentation of the award at the Trenton Senior High School graduation exercises was Mario H. Volpe, the first student of Italian parentage to receive a Trenton Times Scholarship.[16]

In 1936 two Italian American awards were made at the commencement exercises for Trenton Central High School graduates. Mario H. Volpe presented the Unico Club award to Antoinette Christian and Mary Commini.

Amerigo D'Agostino made the Italian Federation of Mercer County award to Jennis Mastrangelo.[17]

On page three of the *Trenton Evening Times* for June 1, 1936 there appeared further evidence of what the Italian Federation of Mercer County was doing to encourage Italian American high school graduates to further their education. The League's education committee presented a gold medal to Miss Carmela Nalbone, a senior at the New Jersey College for Women, who was one of the recipients of a Voorhees Fellowship for advanced study.

Italian American concern focused in 1936 on the run-down condition of the Washington School. In December of 1936 Mario Volpe, representing the P.T.A. of the Washington School, spoke to the Board of Education at its meeting held on December 3, 1936. It is so recorded in the minutes of the Board of Education for December 3, 1936.

The minutes of the Board for January 6, 1938, show that a letter addressed to Mr. Paul Loser, Superintendent of Trenton Schools, was read and filed. It was sent by Paul J. Plumeri, secretary of the Unico Club. It was sent to thank the Board for its foresight "evidenced by the approval of plans for a school building to replace the old Washington School". But by 1938, according to the minutes of the Board of the May 5 meeting, Mario Volpe, representing the P.T.A. of the Washington School, was back before the Board requesting information regarding the probable building of the new Washington School. The delay, it seemed, was caused by the Board's having had to wait to hear from the W.P.A. authorities in Washington, D.C., as to whether the grant might be made. The January 4, 1940, minutes show that the invoices chargeable to PWA Project No. N.J. 1310-F were approved.

Graduation exercises were held at elementary parochial schools. One such in 1936 was for the members of the eighth grade of St. Joachim's School. The Rev. Alfonso Palombi, pastor, presented the diplomas at exercises held in the school auditorium.[18]

The International Institute was again announcing Fall term classes in Italian. Beginners were to meet Tuesday evening with Roland Formidoni as teacher. A new class for those with a slight knowledge of the language was to be taught by Raymond Pane of Rutgers University.[19]

The teaching of Italian had been done since 1910, when St. Joachim's School first opened. When St. James School opened in 1923, Italian was taught there also. But, though the number of Italians in Trenton had been growing and the number of Italian Americans enrolled in Trenton High School had also been growing, the Department of Foreign Languages offered courses only in Latin, French, Spanish, and German. During the twenties many requests were submitted to the Board of Education that Italian be added to the curriculum in the high school. It was not until 1931 that any action was taken. The minutes of the Board for April 1, 1931, record that Italian was to be offered as an additional language for a total of three years

with the opening of the new school building on Chambers Street. The opening was scheduled for September of 1931. The first teacher of Italian was Dr.
Victor Sabary, teacher of Spanish at the high school. The second was Dr.
Robert Lowenstein, who was appointed at the September 7, 1933, meeting
of the Board. The third was Frank Borgia, appointed at the June 6, 1935,
meeting.

War Times

Italian Americans did not forget the land that they had left of their own volition. This was manifested by the names given their organizations: Victor Emmanuel, first king of united Italy; the Bersaglieri, a highly admired branch of the Italian infantry; Camillo Benso Conte di Cavour, revered for his role in the unification of Italy.

But the Italian Americans were now just what "Italian American" implies – Italians of America, and they were loyal to America. Of course, America's 1917-1918 participation in World War I posed no problem for the Italians of America because Italy was one of the allied powers fighting against Germany. Italy's part was played in the northeast of Italy against its traditional enemy, Austria. The Italians boasted proudly that after the disastrous retreat at Caporetto, they came back valorously and forced the capitulation of Austria on November 4, 1918, one week before Germany surrendered to the other allied powers on November 11, 1918.

Some of the items that tell of the Italian American involvement in World War I reveal the various ways in which Trenton's Italian community was active. In 1918, for example, an item appeared in the *Trenton Evening Times* noting that members of the Regina Marguerita Society of the International Institute met on February 26 to hear Miss Bianca Maria Costa of New York City speak in Italian on "Conservation and the Red Cross". Dr. Cubicciotti was scheduled to speak, but because he was unable to attend, Mr. Angelo Ruffo spoke in his stead.[1]

The minutes of the Board of Education for the meeting of May 2, 1918, show that Dr. Charles R. Sista had been called to military duty and that Dr. Samuel Sica was to assume the same duties and services. The daily press later carried the news that Dr. Charles Sista had been given his discharge.[2] In the March 6, 1919, minutes it was recorded that Dr. Sista had submitted an application for re-appointment as Medical Inspector. The newspaper also carried items about the Radice brothers in service, of Girard in France and of William soon to be discharged; and of Daniel A. Spair, who had received his discharge and was to resume practice in the law office of S.L. Katzenbach.[3]

There was community pride shown for the part played by the sons of Italian Americans in the war effort. In November of 1919 the school children of St. Joachim's School tendered a reception and entertainment for the soldiers. The affair was attended by Bishop Thomas J. Walsh. The glee club of 15 girls sang. There was a monologue by Michael Pagano; a duet by Elizabeth Salvatore and Giuseppe Salvatore; a poem to Bishop Walsh by Maria Moretti; quartet selections by Lorenzo Poli, M. Moretti, N. La Ferrara, and A. Carabelli. Seventh grade girls presented a solo by Josephine Salvatore, a mandolin selection by George Pellettieri, a solo by J. Gizzi, and a dialogue by Carmine Ragazzo and Leo Peroni. Adults also took part. There was a trio composed of Mrs. M. Russo, Miss Elizabeth Salvatore, and M.J. Russo; and a monologue in the Roman dialect by Alexander Venanzi. There were also special exercises by groups of boys and the singing of patriotic songs.[4]

There were other observances that were held in honor of Italy's successful termination of its war with and victory over Austria. The Order Sons of Italy, for example, arranged a parade for Sunday, November 16, 1919, featuring the men who had served in both the American and the Italian armies. The soldiers were to parade in uniform to the Pennsylvania Railroad Station, where General Guglielmotti was to be met. A banquet was held at Manze's Hotel at 1 o'clock. At 4 o'clock they were to go to the Trenton High School Auditorium, where the general was to address the audience.[5]

The next day an article regarding the previous day's activities mentioned that General Guglielmotti had thrilled the audience with his speech. Three hundred young men of Italian birth or descent had marched in the parade wearing the uniform of the United States Army. General Guglielmotti had ridden at the head of the column in an automobile with City Commissioner La Barre. With the general on the reviewing stand were Dr. Joseph A. Tempesto, chairman of the celebration committee and other members including Mrs. Santina Radice; Tito Salamandra, treasurer; Angelo Ruffo, Gaetano Di Donato, Antonio Maglione, Vincenzo Lupo, Giorgio Calisti, Maria Fiorello, and Antonio Mengone. The celebration was held under the auspices of the Order Sons of Italy.[6]

In the mid-thirties, Italy's war in Ethiopia occupied the thinking of many Italian Americans, especially those who had been born in Italy. Sanctions had been applied against Italy. Many of the Italian Americans in Trenton had followed the rise of Benito Mussolini in Italy and on the European stage with great interest and pride. In good part this was due to the favorable reports that appeared in the press in the late twenties and early thirties about Mussolini's early social experiments. His words and actions had served to make Italy a nation to be reckoned with. Italian Americans, as a result, were basking in the warmth of what they inferred from press reports. Though many might have deplored Mussolini's war against Ethiopia and his repressive measures in Italy, they nonetheless felt that they should help the Italian cause. I can remember vividly my grandfather's part in this effort. At the time he was operating a modest business distributing and selling peanut oil. His place of business was a storefront on South Clinton Avenue between Bayard and Butler Streets. In order to help circumvent the effects of the sanctions on Italy, he sold very thin sheets of copper of postcard size. Customers would buy the copper cards, write messages on them, and send them to Italy. This was done to help Italy get much-needed copper.

Women were showing their desire to help by turning in their wedding rings to the Italian Red Cross as their contribution. Other efforts were made to help. On March 15, 1936, for example, a benefit for the Italian Red Cross was held in the Trenton Central High School Auditorium. The Colonial Dramatic Club staged *Il Fornaretto di Venezia* (The Little Baker's Boy of Venice). In charge of the committee for the affair were Anthony Carricchia and Vincent Mazzilli.[7] The Independent Order Sons of Italy engaged the Metropolitan Civic Grand Opera Company to present Bizet's "Carmen" at the War Memorial Buiding on March 24, 1936, with proceeds to go to the Italian Red Cross.[8]

There was, of course, strong feeling in this country about the darker side of fascism. But many people misinterpreted the Italian Americans and their feelings. The Italian Americans felt themselves to be true and loyal Americans. America was not involved in Ethiopia, and they felt that they were doing nothing that could be considered as unAmerican. When Italy ultimately won its war, there was great elation felt by many here.

There was a celebration in the city. Among some non-Italians there was apprehension — perhaps even fear — that there might be violence if such a celebration would be allowed to take place. An article in the *Trenton Evening Times* under the headline "Gold Is Exchanged for Steel as Italians Celebrate Conquest" makes clear how unfounded the apprehensions were. The article mentions that "an orderly, colorful celebration was staged in the Memorial Building yesterday by 3000 men, women, and children commemorating Italy's conquest of Ethiopia. The rally was conducted under the auspices of the Italian Red Cross and the Italian World War Veterans".

The article goes on to say that because disorder had been predicted by the American League Against War and Fascism, the city authorities had taken precautions by stationing policemen and detectives around the building. The predicted discorders did not materialize. As for the ceremonies inside the War Memorial Building, the article mentioned that the Rev. Oscar W. Henderson, city councilman, extended greetings on behalf of Mayor William J. Connor to the principal guest, Gaetano Vecchiotti, Italian consular representative stationed in New York City.

There were speeches paying tribute to the soldiers of past and present Italy. The ceremony was marked with the presentation by Commander Vecchiotti of steel wedding bands to about 50 of 500 local women, in replacement of gold rings turned over to the Italian Red Cross in support of its foreign activities. Other rings were to be distributed through the Trenton office of Cav. Felice Ronca, Italian consular agent here. The Rev. Constantine De Santis, assistant pastor of St. Joachim's Church, presided. On the stage there were four tiers of 150 school children of St. Joachim School and of St. James School, each holding alternately a small American and a small Italian flag.[9]

If one can infer from the celebration that a statement was made, it would be that it was not a political statement, but a patriotic one: their allegiance to the United States was not to be questioned, but they could not forget the country of their birth.

With the outbreak of World War II in 1939 and America's active involvement in 1941, matters were completely different: Italy was now an enemy of the United States. America's Italians remained true and firm in their allegiance and loyalty. Many Italian Americans were to be found in the military branches in the various theaters of war, serving loyally and bravely. Those who were sent to Italy went as Americans and were received by the Italians as Americans.

In the latter months of 1940, Italian American organizations began to hold benefits for the American Red Cross. The Roman Society, for example, held a dance in the Roman Hall on November 20 for the benefit of the Red Cross. Atty. Sido Ridolfi was chairman of the committee on arrangements.[10]

Items in the press began to show that there were men going into the United States services. Dr. Alfred J. Barbaro, 1st lieutenant in the Medical Corps, was the assistant chief medical officer at the Trenton induction station. Dr. Frank P. Guidotti, of Trenton, 1st lieutenant, was the chief officer.[11] Anthony J. Sivo, of Butler Street, was a radio mechanic in the Navy, stationed at Norfolk.[12]

Mrs. Mary Olivetti, a "Gold Star" mother of the Auxiliary of Trenton Post No. 2, Italian-American World War Veterans, was honored at a testimonial dinner at the Eldorado Club.[13] Sal G. Angelucci, who recently joined the Army, was given a farewell banquet by the employees of the Trenton Beverage Company.[14] Dr. Frank S. Storaci, member of the 119th Medical Regiment, returned to Trenton from maneuvers in the Carolinas.[15]

On Sunday, December 14, 1941, more than 100 representatives of the 35,000 Americans of Italian extraction in Mercer County met and asserted their "unstinted and unceasing efforts" toward American victory in the war. In a telegram sent the night before to President Roosevelt, the group, which resolved itself into the "Committee of Loyal Americans of Italian Extraction of Mercer County", stated: "The American citizens of the city of Trenton, N.J., and its suburban municipalities, although of Italian parentage, feel it our and their duty, in this hour of trial and worldly disturbance, to express to the people of the United States of America, through you, their unqualified and complete allegiance to this country".

Judge George Pellettieri, of the City District Court, was elected permanent chairman of the committee, with Miss Bertha C. Zoda as the permanent secretary. The group, which made its headquarters at the home of the Italian-American World War Veterans, 344 Hamilton Avenue, donated $500 to the Red Cross Emergency War Relief Fund. Pledges of another $1000 were made.

Dr. Anthony Lettiere headed a committee to urge all 35,000 Americans of Italian extraction to buy defense stamps and bonds. At the meeting, 45 organizations were represented.[16]

At a special monthly meeting of Trenton Lodge No. 701, Order Sons of Italy in America, the assembly unanimously pledged to buy $500 worth of Defense Bonds. The presiding officer asserted that the Order must pledge wholehearted support by giving not only its resources but "lives if necessary" for an ultimate victory against the aggressors.[17]

Trenton Post No. 2, Italian-American World War Veterans, passed a resolution advising Trenton's Defense Council that its members, as well as the Auxiliary, considered it "a privilege to serve in this hour of need", and therefore tendered the unqualified support and services of the body to aid in its valiant efforts to ensure civilian security and protection.[18]

The Columbus Women's Welfare Committee went on record to lend every possible assistance to the Red Cross Emergency Relief Fund. The committee made surgical dressings, knitted and sewed, and also trained in first aid work.[19]

Members of the Italian-American Sportsmen's Club planned a dance to be held Saturday evening, January 17, 1942, the proceeds of which were to be turned over to the Red Cross Emergency War Relief Fund.[20]

At its monthly meeting the Trenton Unico Club received a letter from Joseph V. Zaccone stating: "Along with other civic organizations...our club will be called on for its efforts during the emergency. We do not want to be unprepared".[21] The club pledged wholehearted support to the program of the Local Defense Council and went on record to purchase defense bonds and stamps for the duration.[22]

Upon being elected president of the Unity League, Edmund Lanza urged all members to participate in the sale of defense bonds and savings stamps and to assist in every possible way with the civilian defense of Trenton.[23]

Mrs. Lena Eleuteri, president of the *Societá Romana Femminile*, was in charge of arrangements for the Red Cross Dance which was to benefit the Red Cross War Chest.[24]

Angelo Ruffo, Grand Venerable of the Independent Order Sons of Italy, on February 2, 1942, sent President Roosevelt a resolution adopted by the organization pledging "full support to the government of the United States of America in order to achieve final victory".

Mr. Ruffo informed the President that Article 1 of the order's constitution stated that it was based on "the principles of liberty, equality, and fraternity". He said that it was an association "eminently patriotic, loyal to the United States of America and its institutions and to its constitutional government". The organization purchased $1000 in defense bonds and also sent a check for $15 to the March of Dimes.[25]

The Agabiti Booster Club completed arrangements for its Red Cross benefit to be held at the War Memorial Building on February 23. Miss Florence Perilli was to sing the national anthem. All the proceeds were to go to the Red Cross.[26]

Miss Rhea Cella assisted with plans for a novelty party held Wednesday evening, February 4, 1942, by the Mercer County Committee of Loyal American Women of Italian Extraction. The novelty party was held to benefit the Red Cross War Relief Fund.[27]

On February 28, 1942, Frank A. Vella played the part of a doctor in the play "The Two Orphans", given by an Italian American group in the Trenton Central High School Auditorium on behalf of the Mercer County Chapter of the Red Cross.[28]

A tag day held on May 2, 1942, was sponsored by the Trenton's Service Men's Committee. Joseph Plumeri, a member of the group, stated that proceeds were to be used to purchase gift packages for Trenton's boys in the services.[29]

In May of 1942 a women's first aid class was formed. Mrs. Joseph Pantaleone, chairman of the Red Cross Unit of the Columbus Civic League, had as members of the class the following: Lucy Tartaglia, Theresa Marazzo, Nelli Domanski, Anna Strollo, Ann Suverkrop, Anne Heathcote, Josephine Ferri, Dorothy Kizewski, and Mamie Ridolfi.[30]

Joseph Lucidi, member of the committee arranging the fourteenth annual outing of La Nuova Capitale to be held at the Italian-American Sportsmen's Club, announced that proceeds from the sale of tickets will be donated to the Red Cross War Relief Fund.[31]

Notices of Italian American young men entering the services were appearing regulary in the press. One was especially interesting: four sons of Mr. and Mrs. Samuel Caponey, of 543 South Clinton Avenue, were "serving Uncle Sam": Stephen in the Navy, Samuel Jr. also in the Navy, Corporal John E. in the Army, and Joseph in the Navy.[32]

The following item also occasioned great interest. Francis Caputo, on the occasion of having joined the United States Army and as director of the Office of the Columbus Social Service Center, was tendered a farewell party at the Roman Hall. The Roman Hall was granted for the occasion by Cesare Orsi, president of the Roman Society. Flowers were presented by Anthony Graziano, Chambersburg florist.[33]

Lieut. Sebastian J. Vento, who practiced medicine at 500 Liberty Street, joined the armed forces with a commission as lieutenant. He was stationed at Fort Benning, Georgia.[34]

Club Dinners and Banquets

Among the pleasures most enjoyed were the dinners that were held annually by virtually all Italian American organizations. Such lodges as the *Operaia Savoia* and the *Casteltermini* had purchased halls where their meetings were held, where some members would meet of an evening for cards and wine, and where the annual "banchetto" was held. Other societies would rent these halls for their meetings or for social affairs such as wedding receptions, or they would make use of a public hall such as Nardi's Hall.

We shall now turn to an overview of the many dinners held for one purpose or another that brightened the lives of Trenton's Italian Americans.

In 1911, for example, the Ladies' Auxiliary of St. Joachim's held a spaghetti supper. For this occasion the ladies had decorated the hall with palms and other potted plants. In addition to spaghetti, they served chicken, roast beef, ham, salads, olives, fruits, and other delicacies. A dance followed the dinner. On this occasion the ladies were assisted by the young men of the Parochial Club.[1]

The banquet held at Manze's Hotel on the occasion of General Gugliel-motti's visit to Trenton has already been mentioned.[2]

In 1919 the *Circolo Italiano* held its annual Columbus Day Banquet at their clubhouse at 340 Hamilton Avenue.[3]

In 1921 the Sons of Italy planned big things for the national convention that was held in Trenton. Over 200 delegates were expected to attend. At the customary banquet, held in the Hotel Stacy-Trent, Consular agent Felice Ronca and city officials were present. The executive committee for the convention included Angelo Ruffo, chairman; the Rev. Vincent Serafini, Sigismondo Fantauzzo, and G.R. Cella. The general committee comprised the following lodges and their representatives: *Loggia Meucci* – G.R. Cella, Fabiani Palombi, Nicola Del Gaudio; *Loggia Savoia* – Angela Ruffo, Cesare Ronca, Antonio Selvaggi; *Loggia Washington* – Donato Buchicchio, Angelo Suozzo, Antonio Mengoni; *Loggia Pantaleone* – Vincenzo Fantauzzo, Giuseppe Nalbone; *Loggia Colombo* – A. Mazzetti, N. Masciantoni, P. Scarcioni; *Loggia Adelaide Cairoli* – Signora Santina Radice, Signora Carmela Labella, Signorina Maria Commini; *Loggia Maddalena Carioni* – Signorina Lucietta Aiello, Signorina Giuseppina Cardinale; *Loggia Castelternini* – Agostino Butticé, Domenico D'Amico, Vincenzo Giuliano.[4]

The third Young People's Banquet was held at St. John's Italian Baptist Church in the Social hall. Paul A. Urbani served as toastmaster.[5]

In 1936 Daniel A. Spair was one of the speakers at the annual dinner held by the Kent Athletic Association at the Ewing Riding Academy. Arthur A. Salvatore was toastmaster. Chairman of the affair was Anthony R. Russo.[6]

When the Chambersburg Republican Club planned one of its meetings in 1936, it proposed to feature a spaghetti supper.[7]

At times spaghetti dinners served both as social events and as a means of raising funds for a particular cause or purpose. The Italian-American Sportsmen's Club, for example, ran a spaghetti dinner at its clubhouse for the benefit of the Red Cross in 1937.[8]

In 1937 the Kent Athletic Association held a banquet at the Hotel Stacy-Trent. A floor show was featured and music was furnished by George Quinty and his Cavaliers.[9]

Testimonial dinners also proved to serve at least two purposes: enjoying dinner in the company of friends and honoring a member of the community. Such a dinner was given for Joseph Plumeri, Mercer court interpreter. More than 200 were expected to attend.[10]

The *Societá Romana di Mutuo Soccorso* honored Dr. Albert F. Moriconi at a testimonial dinner-dance held at the Italian-American Sportsmen's Club in 1937. Sylvester Stella was chairman of the affair, which was attended by more than 250 guests.[11]

The Bayard Social Club held its third annual banquet on October 27, 1937. President Anthony Graziano had named Dr. James Rita and Dr. Gennaro Cardelia co-chairmen of the committee which was made up of John Fratticolli, Robert Curini, Americo Trotto, Joseph Stanzione, George Carnevale, Frank Graziano, and Charles Valenzia.[12]

The Model Social Club held its fourth annual dinner-dance at the Knights of Columbus Hall on November 17, 1937. Frank T. Pesce, chairman, was assisted by Paul Martine, Michael Peters, and Frank Romano.[13]

In 1938 James Eppolito, president, was tendered a testimonial dinner on March 24 by members of the 7th Ward Democratic Club at the Princeton Inn. Vincent Panaro served as toastmaster. Speeches and entertainment were featured.[14]

On May 11 of the same year Remigio Ugo Pane, instructor of a class in Italian at the International Institute, was guest of honor at a dinner at Nobili's Restaurant. Alfred C. Gregory presented a gold chain on behalf of the class members. It was announced that Mr. Pane had been granted an assistant professorship in the Department of Romance Languages at Rutgers University.[15]

It was also customary in those days to honor young men or women who had recently received college or university degrees. Vincent Girard, who was in the graduating class of 1938 at State Teachers College, was guest at a dinner-dance held in the Hotel Hildebrecht by the Hamilton Social Club. Arthur A. Salvatore acted as toastmaster. Samuel Faggella was the committee chairman.[16]

A gala dinner was held for a very special occasion, the celebration of the dedication of the Roman Hall in October of 1939, already mentioned in another section.

In 1940 the Roman Society held a testimonial banquet in its own building in honor of the Society's founders. Those to be honored were Francesco Di Marco, Vincenzo Venanzi, Pietro Eleuteri, Antonio Innocenzi, Nicola Innocenzi, Daniel Bentivoglia, Ottavio Jachetti, and Domenico Vannozzi. Alexander Venanzi was toastmaster, and the principal speaker was Dr.. Albert F. Moriconi. At the time the Roman Society, with a membership of some 500, was the largest Italian society in Trenton. It had a ladies' auxiliary of some 300 members.[17]

The Trenton Unico Club over the years held a number of dinners. In 1940 Samuel P. Guidotti was chairman of the committee that arranged for the annual May dinner-dance at the Hotel Stacy-Trent.[18]

In August of 1940 the Roman Society observed its forty-fourth anniversary with the most elaborate celebration in the unit's history. A banquet and ceremonial exercises, with entertainment and dancing, were held in the society's home on Whittaker Avenue. Sylvester Stella was toastmaster.[19]

Trenton Lodge No. 701 of the Order Sons of Italy in America held a commemorative dinner-dance on December 8, 1940, in the Roman Hall to celebrate the 20th anniversary of its founding. Joseph Gruerio acted as toastmaster.[20]

Russell Lupo was guest of honor Sunday evening, January 26, 1941, at a dinner given by the Villalba Society in the organization's auditorium. Joseph Plumeri, president of the society, was toastmaster.[21]

On February 22, 1941, the Old Guard Club held a Washington's Birthday dinner at their clubrooms, at 159 Hamilton Avenue. John Russo of Brooklyn delivered an address. The toastmaster was Joseph Brenna. The chairman of the committee on arrangements was Philip Di Risi.[22]

An "April Shower" dinner-dance was one of five social events scheduled by the Trenton Unico Club for the year 1941. Peter W. Radice was named chairman of the entertainment committee.[23]

Frank Fidanza, president of St. Gabriel's Society of St. James R.C. Church and of the Italian-American Social Club of North Trenton, was feted on Sunday, April 22, 1941, by fellow members of the Villalba Society at a dinner held in the Villalba Hall.[24]

In October of 1941, Gaetano Albanese, 80 years old and the oldest member of the Casteltermini Society, was honored at a banquet given by the society. About 400 persons attended. Vincent Giuliano was chairman of the committee on arrangements.[25]

On January 25, 1942, Joseph Mainiero was tendered a testimonial dinner by the Villalba Society at its clubrooms. Angelo J. Lupo was chairman of the committee arranging the affair.[26]

Miss Mary Malagrino was chairman of the Debonair Girls' third annual dinner party that was held on March 7, 1942.[27]

The Unity League held its seventh annual dinner-dance at the Hotel

Hildebrecht on February 28. Peter J. Fiabane chaired the committee that was in charge of arrangements.[28]

Dr. Anthony J. Lettiere was chairman of the committee arranging for the testimonial dinner held in honor of the Rev. Emilio A. Cardelia, pastor of St. Joachim's Church, on April 26, 1942, in the Roman Hall.[29]

A farewell dinner was given for the Rev. Salvatore C. Shangler by the congregation of the Immanuel Presbyterian Church on Monday, April 20 at Fisher's Inn. Richard Leoni served as both committee chairman and as toastmaster.[30]

Dr. Joseph Pantaleone was the principal speaker at a dinner celebrating the anniversary of the Giovanni Bovio Lodge on Sunday, August 30, 1942, at Bonanni's Cafe.[31]

The Immanuel Presbyterian Church sponsored a fellowship dinner on Thursday, November 12 at 7 p.m. at the church. The Young Ladies' Guild was in charge.[32]

Under the auspices of the Joy Club, a spaghetti supper was served at the Club Eldorado. Mrs. Rose Salvante was chairman of the committee in charge of arrangements.[33]

The annual rabbit and pheasant banquet of the Italian-American Sportsmen's Club was held on Sunday, November 22, 1942, at 12:30 p.m. in the club auditorium. Dancing followed the dinner. Elmer Dal Corso was chairman of the committee.[34]

Just for Fun

By the end of the 1930s we find that many organizations were being formed purely for the purpose of making entertainment or social gatherings possible. In the first two decades of this century most of the activities that provided amusement for the Italian immigrants stemmed from their churches and various church organizations. By the end of 1929 there were 91 incorporated organizations. Though these made possible a number of social activities, their basic purposes were to satisfy the need for mutual aid and to weld these new citizens or prospective citizens into political groups that might carry some clout. As early as 1902 there was a social club — the Young Italian Progressive and Social Club; by 1907 there was a dramatic club — the Juvenile Dramatic Circle; by 1916 there was the Tripoli Social Club. The *Dante Lyceum* represented a culture group. There were also the beginnings of athletic or hunting clubs. But getting together simply to enjoy the company of others and to provide such pleasure and entertainment as dances, for example, made possible was not to come about widely until the 1930s. What follows will show what all types of groups were doing — just for fun.

In October of 1931 a Hallowe'en Dance was held in the St. James Hall. Arrangements for it were made by a committee consisting of Mary Petruccio, Helen Galardo, Mary Paulinton, Virginia Ribarara, Josephine Bosso, and Edith Puliti.[1]

In the following month, the Ever Ready Club of the International Institute planned a dance. Nellie Marini was one of those in charge of the affair.[2]

The International Y Boys' Club held a Christmas Party in 1934. Nicholas Dondiego provided the music and featured Gasper Fantauzzo, mandolin; Samuel San Filippo, trumpet; and Ernest Zampisi, harmonica.[3]

Under the auspices of the Italian Federation of Mercer County, a card party was held in 1935. Anna R. Faggella was in charge.[4]

Another such organization to run a dance was the Unity League. On June 4 the affair took place in the Eldorado Hall.[5]

In 1936 the Melrose Club sponsored a dance on February 4. Virginia Corallo was the general chairman. She was assisted by Samuel Nalbone.[6]

The Young Ladies' Sodality of St. Joachim's Church held a Pre-Lenten Card Party. The committee was chaired by Adele Palombi.[7]

In 1936 the Italian-American Independent Club of North Trenton held its third annual outing at Eggerts Crossing. General chairman Alex Farina was assisted by Patsy Caserta.[8]

In 1937 the Young Ladies' Sodality of St. Joachim's Church held a barn dance. Fannie De Paola, chairman, was assisted by Mamie Rita.[9]

Also in 1937, a dinner-dance was held by the Model Social Club. The chairman for the affair was Frank T. Pesce. He was assisted by Paul Martine, Michael Peters, and Frank Romano.[10]

A novelty dance was held by the Ladies' Auxiliary of the North Trenton Italian-American Social Club. Catherine Pontrella assisted with the arrangements.[11]

In 1938 the Italian-American Ladies' Social Club sponsored a novelty party. The president of the club was Rose Chiacchio. Irene Felcone assisted with preparations.[12]

A Social Thursday Evening was held by the Sportswoman Club in Caiazzo's Hall. Frances Tugni, club president, was aided by Mrs. Mark Fuccello.[13]

A balloon dance was given by the Young Ladies' Sodality of St. Joachim's Church. The affair was held in the St. Joachim School auditorium. Ruth De Rosa assisted with arrangements.[14]

In 1939 the Atlas Club held its annual dance on November 29 in the ballroom of the War Memorial Building. Joseph Riggi, chairman, was assisted by Blacy Immordino, Russell Radice, Frank Seamone, Frank Rotunda, Steve Cacciatore, Carl Dellaira, and Joseph Lombardo. Robert B. Immordino was president of the club.[15]

In 1941 the Roman Society held a dance in the Roman Ballroom. Two orchestras had been engaged for the evening's entertainment.[16]

In February of 1941 the Atlas Girls' Club held a Valentine skating party at the Garden Skating Rink. Parmena Sciandra served as chairman of the arrangements committee.[17]

The Unico Club of Trenton made plans for their April Shower Dinner-Dance. Peter W. Radice was chairman of the entertainment committee.[18]

The Ladies' Auxiliary of Trenton Post No. 2, Italian-American World War Veterans of the United States held their first annual dance. Elsie Jachetti assisted with preparations.[19]

A week's vacation at the Worthington Hotel in Atlantic City was planned by the Damselettes. Officers of the club were Pauline Biondi, president; Ada Campana, vice president; Chris Angeline, secretary; and Rose Di Biagio, treasurer.[20]

Also in 1941 the Damselettes held a skating party on November 19 at the White City Skating Rink. Lucie Russo assisted with arrangements.[21]

The Master Social Club held its first annual dance in the War Memorial Building on December 17, 1941. Armando D. Ricci was one of the committee members.[22]

In 1942 the third annual dinner party was held by the Debonair Girls on March 7. Mary Malagrino chaired the committee on arrangements.[23]

This section closes with mention of another type of amusement indulged in by a number of men in the late 1930s – the spoof or gentle satire. They called themselves the Hamilton Avenue Protective Association and the

South Clinton Mutual Aid Society. One such occasion was billed as their sixty-third annual dinner. Featured was Salvatore Scardone, who was the well known and highly regarded creator of the fireworks displays which were the culmination of the saints' festivals. He was also appreciated as something of a wag and at times was himself the object of satire. "Professor" Scardone was "to tell tales" of sunny Italy at the dinner held in Allegretti's Cafe. On such occasions he would be attired formally in topper and tails and driven to the dining hall in a cortege of automobiles.[24]

In the News

With the exception of what appears in the sections on work and on politics, for the most part attention has been given to the activities of groups or of organizatons. One is not to infer from this, however, that Italian Americans were not participating in matters that were of an individual or of a non-Italian nature. Italian Americans were beginning to appear in the local press as individuals. They were participating in the life of the broader community of Trenton well outside the Italian enclaves.

In 1904, for example, Pasquale Dileo appeared in a human interest feature published in the *Trenton Times*. The headline read "Prince of Bootblacks Discusses Some Past Mayors". The article is interesting not only for the observations made by "the Prince" but also for the flavor which the verbatim report imparted.[1]

The Italian American business man began to advertise. The *Trenton Times* carried an ad run by Joe Graziano, the self-styled cut-price Cigar Man of 114 Perry Street. He touted his cigars by claiming "A Fire is necessary that my goods may be appreciated".[2]

That Italian Americans were taking enthusiastically to American sports can be seen by a sports notice on August 30, 1907. The headline reads "Marolda Eased Up; Pennington Won." It went on to record "Bases on balls: Marolda; Struck out by Marolda, 6."

Young women also made the sports columns. In 1918 under the headline "Two Hard Games by T.H.S. Girls", the following appeared as team members: Phillipena Franzoni, of the Senior Team; and Philomena Graziano, of the Junior Team.[3] The love affair with baseball and basketball was well under way.

Among the pugilists still remembered are Young Angelo and Kid Emmons. In 1919 Young Angelo, the featherweight, told the *Times* reporter that he accepted the "defi" issued by Kid Emmons.[4]

In 1919 the name La Guardia was already in the local news. Richard D. La Guardia, industrial secretary of the Y.M.C.A., was promoting a fire prevention campaign.[5]

Another Italian American who had achieved local prominence was Donato Pierro. In 1919 an article about him appeared under the headline "Prominent Italian Had Varied Career. City Contractor Arrived with 35 Cents in His Pockets." The article went on to mention that Pierro had conducted a banking business and a steamship ticket agency; he had also been involved in the wholesale grocery business. He gave up these enterprises to become a contractor. He had been one of the incorporators of the Evangelical Presbyterian Church on Whittaker Avenue.[6]

We begin to see the advertising of Italian restaurants. An ad in 1919 for the Roma Restaurant at 12 North Warren Street mentioned special cookery; *table d'hote* and *a la carte.*[7]

Engagement and wedding announcements began quite early. By 1911 an announcement for the wedding of Miss Louise Catherine Camera appeared.[8] By 1919 such announcements were already quite common. Report of the marriage of Charles Paglione and Miss Mary Benedetti, with photographs, appeared on November 19.[9]

In 1923 an item appeared naming Joseph Plumeri as a member of the Advertising and Publicity Committee of the Trenton Real Estate Board.[10]

Italian Americans had been vying for city jobs. In 1926 among those who passed examinations as announced by the Civil Service Commission were the following: Anthony De Angelo, Anthony F. Di Louie, and Albert Mastrangeli, for the Police Department; Anthony De Angelo, Daniel T. Tomasulo, Anthony Di Louie, and Albert Mastrangeli for the Fire Department.[11]

In March of 1929 Gustave Napolean was shown by photograph in an advertisement for Pertussin, a cough remedy, as a popular Trenton druggist at Whittaker Avenue and Mott Street.[12]

Miss Acile Bozano in 1931 was chairman of a group in charge of window decorations for the celebration marking the fiftieth anniversary or Golden Jubilee Week of the Girl Reserves of the Y.W.C.A.[13]

An Italian American who achieved more than local prominence was Joseph Schiavone. His obituary appeared in November of 1931. At the time of his death he was president of the International Exchange Bank in Washington, D.C. The obituary mentioned that on his coming to the United States, he had settled in Trenton. He took a course at Rider College and secured a position in the Mechanics Bank. After some 20 years he resigned his positon to go to Washington as assistant secretary to U.S. Senator James E. Martine. He studied law, published a newspaper, and founded the International Bank. During World War I he served as secretary of the information bureau of the Italian Embassy in Washington.[14]

By 1939 Benedict Napoliello was entertaining the citizens of Trenton as leader of the Municipal Band at Sunday summer concerts held in Cadwalader Park.[15]

In 1937 at a meeting of the Master Barbers' Assn., the following officers were installed: Michael Shema, president; Frank Martarano, vice president; Anthony De Lia, secretary; Paul Gagliardi, recording secretary; Sebastian Castranova, treasurer; Pat Seppia, sergeant at arms. Committee chairmen were named: Ralph Di Donato, publicity; Ivo Sebastiani, sympathy.[16]

Louis P. Marciante, president of the State Federation of Labor, in 1937, "Hit claims by the CIO" and charged that "Front Page" methods had been used.[17]

In 1938 Benedict Napoliello was conducting the Eagle Philharmonic Band at Cadwalader Park Summer Concerts. On August 7 the band program featured sopranos Miss Florence Perilli and Miss Rhea Cella.[18]

Frank Locane, committee chairman, arranged for the third annual outing of the employees of the Princeton Worsted Mills. Miss Angela Calisti and Peter Grosso were committee members.[19]

On Sunday, August 21, Benedict Napoliello's band concert featured operatic and classical compositions. Soloists at the concert were Miss Rhea Cella, soprano, and Joseph Siciliano, tenor.[20]

Miss Phyllis Radice took part in a piano recital presented in the Carroll Robbins School auditorium by pupils of Mrs. Joseph Radice, mother of Phyllis.[21]

Miss Willa Greco was a member of the committee arranging the sixth annual banquet which was given by the Trenton Evening High School Alumni Association. Anthony E. Carvale was the general chairman.[22]

Thomas Frascella, president of Local 1356 of the Longshoremen's Union, and Rudolph Snorski, member of the local executive board, attended the four-day wage conference in New York City as Trenton representatives.[23]

According to the Civil Service Commission, in 1939 among 75 eligible for appointment as institutional instructor in tailoring were Joseph S. Fradusco, Anthony Rebecca, and Ignazio Ferrara.[24]

Miss Maline Di Franco, active member of the Three M Club of the Y.M.C.A., read the constitution at a meeting held in the association building.[25]

Trenton barbers attended the first annual convention of the Associated Master Barbers of New Jersey held at New Brunswick. Guests included members of the N.J. Licensing Board Martin Gasparini, Anthony Danza, and Charles Pagliuca; and International Representative of the Journeymen's Union Charles La Motta.[26]

Miss Eda Epifanio assisted with the first of a series of folk art evenings at the International Institute.[27]

Miss Florence Modina assisted with plans for a Holiday Hop given by the Citadel Club of the Y.W.C.A. in the association auditorium.[28]

Miss Lucy Formicola was in charge of arrangements for the dance given by the Coed Social Club of the Y.W.C.A. in the association building.[29]

Mrs. August Anselmi served as one of the hostesses at the novelty party sponsored by the Ladies' Auxiliary 540, Bus Drivers Union, in the Chambers Street clubrooms.[30]

Frank Acolia was elected as the new president of the Trenton Traffic Club.[31]

Joseph V. Lupo was feted at a dinner at Palumbo's Cafe in Philadelphia given by the employees of a Camden supermarket, of which he was general manager.[32]

Angelo Giambelluco chaired the committee which arranged for a trip to the New York World's Fair, sponsored by the Atlantic Products Corp. for its 175 employees.[33]

Morris Malmignati was business manager of Local 225 of the United Paper, Toy, and Novelty Workers of America, CIO, which was holding its second annual banquet in the Roman Hall.[34]

Louis Dottini, former member of the Provincetown Players of New York, directed the Trenton Players Club's presentation of "See Naples and Die".[35]

Miss Josephine Salvatore, contralto and a member of the Trenton Opera Association, was a guest artist at the sacred musicale presented by the senior choir of the Central Methodist Church in the church sanctuary.[36]

Maury Salamandra, secretary of the Approved Umpires Association, served as chairman of the A.U.A.'s annual banquet.[37]

Leonard Vecchiola was chairman of the entertainment committee of Trenton Aerie, No. 100, Fraternal Order of Eagles, which made plans for the St. Patrick's Day Party held at the Eagles' home on North Warren Street.[38]

A get-together dance was sponsored under the auspices of the Ladies' Garment Workers Union. Among those serving on the committee for arrangements were Miss Marian Tulamello, Miss Jennie Bruno, Andrew De Paolo, and Milo Tramantana.[39]

Joseph Catana and Michael Donofrio were among those arranging a sports and entertainment program for the annual outing given by the Trenton Aerie No. 100, Fraternal Order of Eagles.[40]

Mrs. Violet Amati conducted the program at the meeting of the Trenton Chapter, No. 145, Women of the Moose held on Friday, September 19, 1941, at the Moose Home.[41]

Initiation ceremonies were held by the Trenton Aerie, No. 100, Fraternal Order of Eagles on Sunday, September 21, 1941. Among those installed were Leonard Vecchiola, Worthy President, and Joseph Calderone, secretary.[42]

Peter A. Pulone assisted with the plans for a testimonial dinner given to honor Walter D. Cougle, district WPA director, at Bonanni's Cafe. A large number of other representatives of labor unions were to attend.[43]

An item appeared announcing a six-dollar boost in wages for workers at the Aurele M. Gatti Co., at 524 E. Washington Street, one of the largest manufacturers of jewels for precision instruments in the United States.[44]

In 1942 George Posta served as chairman of the entertainment committee for the Mercer County Pharmaceutical Association's sixth annual dinner-dance at Leghorn Farms. Reynold Salvatore served as a member of the committee.[45]

Mrs. Elizabeth Episcopo was chairman of the spaghetti dinner committee of the United Democratic Clubs of Mercer County held at the Eldorado Club. She was assisted by Mrs. Theresa Fabrizio. This affair was the first of its kind held by this group. They expected to serve 800 persons.[46]

Dr. Anthony J. Lettiere was the guest of honor at a testimonial dinner held by the Medical Journal Club because he had passed the examination given by the American Board of Surgery.[47]

Leonard Vecchiola, chairman of the entertainment committee of Trenton Aerie, No. 100, Fraternal Order of Eagles, was preparing the annual outing for more than 1700 active Eagle members and their families. Assisting on various committees were Al Pone, Joseph Catana, Al Cacciatore, Michael Donofrio, Harry Catana, and Tony Lizzano.[48]

Miss Theresa Coltre assisted with plans for the Hallowe'en Dance held at the Roman Hall under the auspices of the U.E. Local 119. The chairman of the committee was Joseph Vizzini.[49]

Other Cultural Activities

The culture of a people may be seen as the total of their language, religious practices, tools, organizations, and so on. But very often the term culture is used somewhat narrowly to denote practice of the various arts. It is with this aspect of the Italian American community that we will now deal.

If we consider their social needs and organizations as perhaps the earliest manifestations of their culture, we may find considerable evidence in the list of organizations already examined. Though at the very beginning, in 1886, the basic, and perhaps most important, factor causing the immigrants to band together was the need to provide mutual aid, we can detect additional concerns. The Italian has a reverence for learning. It is not surprising, then, to find that very soon the purposes of the organizations began to list more than mutual aid as their purpose for founding an organization. The words educational, intellectual, patriotic, and recreative are found with ever greater frequency in the statements of purposes on incorporation papers.

From 1899, the year in which the Italian Democratic Club of N.J. was incorporated, we begin to find some of the above-mentioned words. The purposes of this club were stated as social, recreative, promotive of the literary advancement of its members and of the principles of the Democratic Party.

Two of the early groups whose activities were in the performing arts which could be enjoyed by the community at large were the Mascagni Italian Band and the Neapolitan Juvenile Dramatic Club, both organized in 1907. The dramatic groups were especially effective in providing entertainment, and a number of these were organized over the years. The "City of Naples" Dramatic Club was founded in 1917, the *Circolo Filodrammatico Enrico Caruso* in 1922, the *Circolo Filodrammatico Gabriele D'Annunzio* in 1922, the *Circolo Filodrammatico Felice Cavallotti* in 1924, and the *Circolo Filodrammatico Casteltermini* in 1935.

One of the sad aspects of an undertaking such as this overview is that very little remains of written records of these organizations and their productions. A few persons recall something of what was done. Alfonso Bilancio is one of these. He remembers the staging of *Il Moro di Venezia* Italian for *Othello*. Fortunately an item in the *Trenton Evening Times* tells us that this play was presented in the auditorium of the Trenton Central High School under the auspices of the Welfare Committee of the Italian Federation of Mercer County. It was done by the *Circolo Filodrammatico Coloniale*, founded in 1935. Angelo Salerno, well-known in the Italian colony for past successes in directing Italian drama, was in charge. The cast was as follows: Desdemona, Signorina Catarina Zucchetti; Otello, Giuseppe Maisto; Il Doge and Ludovico, Felice Caracciolo; Brabanzio, Michele Campo; Graziano, Nicola Capone; Cassio, Michele D'Addio; Iago, Giuseppe Pica; Emilia, Signora Santina Radice; Rodrigo, Giuseppe Marrazzo; Montano, Nicola Capasso; Secondo Ufficiale, Rocco Pagano.

In the tradition of a much earlier time, a comedy sketch was also presented. It was played by Alessandro (Ziggy) Venanzi, Anna Masciantoni, Domenico Torlini, and Angelo Salerno.[1]

It is interesting to note that two of the players, Giuseppe Pica and Giuseppe Marrazzo, were two of the four trustees of the four named in the incorporation paper.

Giuseppe Maisto had been active in Italian dramatics in Trenton since 1907, when he was listed as one of the trustees of the Neapolitan Juvenile Dramatic Circle. He was so much a lover of drama and he revered William Shakespeare so greatly that he named two sons Hamlet and Othello, and two daughters Ophelia and Desdemona.

Alfonso Bilancio recalls that other plays produced were *Hamlet* and *La Tosca*. He also remembers that farces featuring Domenico Russo as Pulcinella were very well received.

On Saturday, February 28, 1942, a performance of the seven-act drama *The Two Orphans of Paris* was presented in the auditorium of Trenton Central High School by the New Colonial Dramatic Club.[2] Those who took part were Joseph Marazzo, Joseph Pica, Nick Capasso, Mike D'Addio, Mike Campo, Felice Caracciolo, Antonio Vella, Aniello Gervasio, Emilio Petrecca, Frank Piraino, Alfredo Mottola, Angelo Belviso, Simone Caruso, Mrs. Lina Eleuteri, Mrs. Lina De Marco, Mrs. Zoe Marini, Miss Lillian Palmieri, Miss Emily Angeletti, Miss Lola Forcone, Miss Rosa Moscato, Miss Rosa Perroni, and Miss Jenny Flagiella.

We have seen in the records of St. Joachim's Church that as early as 1915 the play *College Chums* was one of the activities provided by the church. The records also include the Nativity and Passion plays, both given by Sicilian groups, and the Nativity play given by the Neapolitans.

The parishioners of St. James R.C. Church had such theatrical groups as the Chianese Dramatic Company and the Granese Company, both of Philadelphia, come to give performances in the school auditorium. The records of St. James Church show that the plays *Chitarra Romana, 'O Festino e la Legge, O' Miracolo D'a Madonna* were given. They also had the Conte Luna group of New York City present the play *Cuore di Madre* in March of 1940.[3] St. Anne's Society of St. James R.C. Church presented the drama *Reginella Campagnola* in 1940.[4]

In 1939 the *Societá Romana di M.S.* presented Angelo Gloria and his company in the Trenton Central High School auditorium, to raise money for their building fund.[5]

Church groups were giving religious plays such as *Mary Magdala*. This was presented in St. Joachim's auditorium on April 10, 1938.[6]

The Italian Americans from Campania, of which Naples is a part, relied on companies from New York City for singers, comics, and dramatic artists. One of those from Campania was Antonio Vigliano, who came to Trenton on May 2, 1914, from his hometown Grumo Nevano, which is near Naples. He was born on October 2, 1895. He had been a barber in Italy, and on his arrival he had a trade he could rely on. After World War I, he was a barber in the Hotel Sterling for 12 years before going into business for himself.

He played guitar and mandolin, and he sang Neapolitan songs. He formed his own orchestra and played at gala testimonial dinners for such well-know persons as Sido Ridolfi and Armando Conti. He is still a member of the Trenton Musicians Association Local 62.

Mr. Vigliano was a member of the *Circolo Filodrammatico Città di Napoli*, circa 1917-1918. This group prepared and presented skits in the Neapolitan dialect. Most of their performances were staged in the Hungarian Hall and in St. Joachim's School auditorium.

He remembers engaging Gennaro Gardenia, singer and actor in Neapolitan plays, and Gennaro Amato, comic actor in the Neapolitan dialect. Both of these men were directors of *La Compagnia Filodrammatica Napoletana*, in New York City. They were very popular and came to Trenton three or four times a year during the 1930s.

Mr. Vigliano was the producer and director of Perrucci's *La Cantata dei Pastori*, the Nativity play loved by the Neapolitans. It was given in the St. Joachim school auditorium in December of 1928. Only a partial list of the members of the cast could be gleaned from the memory of the few remaining who had taken part in the production. The cast included: St. Joseph, Antonio Cipullo; the Blessed Mother, Maria Ferrante; the Angel, John Conte; Armente a shepherd, Anthony Vella; Armente's son, Mario Volpe; Razzullo, a comic, Domenico Russo; Sarchiapone, a comic, Raffaele Volpe; and a fisherman, Michael D'Addio.

Nicholas Capasso, like Mr. Vigliano, was very active in the local dramatic group, *Il Circolo Filodrammatico Coloniale*. He is a native of Trenton, having been born at 54 Mott Street on September 13, 1912. Not only does he have remarkable recall but he has among his memorabilia a sword he used in the play *La Tragedia di Sant'Antimo* ("The Tragedy of St. Antimo"), photographs, fragments of books of plays which they staged, and a few of the programs printed for the performances. The following were plays staged by the drama club: *Una Notte a Firenze* ("A Night in Florence"), a historical drama in three acts; *Il Bastardo; Margherita Pusteria ovvero La Terribile Notte di San Giovanni del 1341* ("Margaret Pusteria, or the Terrible Night of St. John 1341"), a play in six acts; *Il Favorito della Regina* ("The Queen's Favorite"); *Il Sonnambulo*

ossia Il Segno Punitore ("The Sleep-walker, or The Punitive Sign"), a play in
three acts; *I Due Segreti* ("The Two Secrets"), a farce by Milesville translated
from the French by Gaetana de Cesari Rosa; *Il Ritorno del Galeotto* ("The
Return of the Convict"); *Bozzetto Napoletano* ("Neapolitan Skit"), a farce; *La
Tragedia di Sant'Antimo*. Mr. Capasso mentioned that the Liceo Dante had
staged *The Count of Monte Cristo* in 1918.

The Sicilians were also active in dramatics. They produced a Nativity
play, *La Pastorale*. The minutes of the Board of Education for the meeting of
November 7, 1935, show that the Circolo Filodrammatico Casteltermini
rented the auditorium of the Trenton Central High School for entertainment
to be held December 15. Mary Fantauzzo De Bono, daughter of Sigismondo
Fantauzzo who helped to produce and stage "La Pastorale", asserts that
December 15 was the date set for the play. Mr. Fantauzzo had served in the
same capacity in his home town of Casteltermini. Mary De Bono remembers
that the following took part: St. Joseph, Joseph Ballone; the Angel, Dominic
Di Balsi; the Devil, Antonio Scannella; the Shepherd, Carmelo Fantauzzo;
and Death, Joseph Schillace. The same group staged *La Pastorale* in the St.
James Hall the following year. Mr. Scannella was aptly chosen to play the
Devil as he was by trade a blacksmith. His smithy was on Swan Street, and I
remember as a boy looking into the blackness of the smithy to see the
sparks fly as the tall, burly, ruddy-faced smith pounded away at glowing
iron. I remember, too, that our evenings at home were filled with the minute
details regarding these plays which both Mr. Volpe and Mr. Fantauzzo
reported. Both were very close and dear friends of ours who visited us
every evening of the week.

What is interesting about these Nativity plays is that their roots go back to
the middle ages and the mystery plays, "mystery" because they dealt with
matter taken from the New Testament. It is interesting to note, too, that they
contain touches of the *Commedia dell'Arte* in that the cast spoke standard
Italian, but the comics in both plays spoke in their native dialect; for example
Sarchiapone and Razzullo spoke in the Neapolitan dialect.

Other cultural programs were prepared and performed; those by children
were held to be especially delightful. In June of 1910, for example, an
interesting Children's Day Program was rendered by the Italian Presbyterian
Church on Whittaker Avenue on Sunday evening, June 19. Featured were
musical instrument selections, singing by individuals and choruses, poetry
reading, and recitations. The article noted that the children were all Italian
– even those named Fisher, their parents had probably borne the name of
Pesce, Italian for fish.[7]

In 1938 a professional magic and vaudeville show was given in St.
Joachim's Auditorium. It was billed as a "Night of Mystery and Entertainment". Among the performers was Mitchell Mastrangelo, who appeared
as "Little Bobby Breen".[8]

In April of 1940 an accordion concert featuring a 25-piece band and two soloists was presented in the Roman Hall.[9]

Out-of-town talent, as has been noted, was called on. In November of 1936 the Italian-American Sportsmen's Club arranged for both an afternoon and an evening of entertainment in the Trenton Central High School Auditorium. The program was billed as an all-star vaudeville show which was presented by the Italian Broadcasting System of Allentown, Pa. The vaudeville performers were listed as opera singers, comedians, radio stars, and dancers in costume.[10]

In 1936 the *Sunday-Times Advertiser* ran an item-announcing that, under the auspices of the Independent Order Sons of Italy, the opera "Carmen" was to be staged in March at the War Memorial Building by the Metropolitan Civic Grand Opera Company.[11]

Other types of programs of cultural interest such as lectures were planned. In September of 1921, for example, under the auspices of the Italian Club and other Italian societies of Trenton, elaborate exercises were held to commemorate the sixth centennial of the death of Dante Alighieri, the greatest of Italy's poets. The program was held in the Trenton High School Auditorium. Addresses were delivered by Agostino Di Biasi, editor of the *Italian Review of New York City*, and by Professor G. McLean Harper, professor of English literature at Princeton University. Dr. J.A. Tempesto presided. The addresses were followed by a musical program.[12]

Another such occasion was the Virgilian Commemoration held on December 28, 1930, under the auspices of the Trenton Unico Club in the Trenton High School Auditorium. The main addresses were delivered by Dr. Leopoldo Vaccaro, eminent Philadelphia surgeon and Virgilian scholar, and by Professor Domenico Vittorini, of the University of Pennsylvania, an authority on Dante. Included was a musical program by Miss Louise Masino, soprano, accompanied by Miss Splendora Leone, and piano solos by Miss Leone.

The committee in charge was as follows: Dr. Joseph Pantaleone, chairman; Salvatore Marinari, Albert Dal Corso, Angelo Falzone, Samuel Colletti, Frank Ciruzzi, and Michael A. Carlucci. A sub-committee of Italian teachers assisted. They were as follows: Miss Helen D'Acquili, Miss Angelina Petrino, Miss Louise D'Acquili, Miss Mary Moretti, Miss Theresa Petrino, Miss Jennie Acquaviva, Miss Erzia Pernazza, Miss Mildred Carlucci, Miss Marie Acquaviva, and Miss Marie Cerone. Several members of the Italian Business and Professional Men's Club aided with the arrangements.[13]

In May of 1938, under the auspices of the Italian Culture Circle, a lecture, "Both Italys in Spain", was delivered by Randolph Pacciardi, noted lawyer and author, editor and lecturer of Paris on a speaking tour of America, in the Hungarian National Home, Genesee and Hudson Streets. The speech was delivered in Italian.[14]

Another aspect of the Italian American culture was to be seen in the newspapers published in Trenton. For many years these were written solely in Italian, but by the late 1920s one finds that English was also being used. The earliest of the Italian newspapers to be published in Trenton was *La Sentinella*, from 1905 to 1911. Its publishers were Ronca and Samelli at 686 South Clinton Avenue. Next came *La Battaglia*, publishec by Joseph Schiavone at 528 Hudson Street from 1912 to 1914. The third to appear was *L'Italo-Americano*, with Pasquale Frallicciardi as editor at 316 Hudson Street, from 1912 to 1930. In 1917 *Il Secolo XX* was published with Armando Perilli as editor at 120 Mott Street, 1917 to 1930. *Il Bollettino del Popolo*, with Attilio Perilli as editor at 482 Chestnut Avenue, appeared in 1923 and ran until 1927. Next came *La Capitale*, with Joseph Mainiero as editor at South Clinton and Hamilton Avenues. It ran from 1927 to 1928.

With *Americanism* a new trend came – the regular use of English as the basic language. It called itself a quadri-lingual weekly, *i.e.,* it was published in Hungarian, Polish, Italian, and English. It was published by the La Guardia Publishing Company: Irene La Guardia, Publisher; Marie La Guardia, Business Manager; and Richard La Guardia, Consulting Editor. This first appeared in 1928. Then came *La Nuova Capitale*, Italian and English Weekly, Joseph Mainiero editor at 505 South Clinton Avenue, from 1930. The last was *The Italian Journal*, with Amerigo D'Agostino as editor, at 213 E. Hanover Street, from 1932 to 1933.[15]

These weeklies did not constitute all that Trenton's Italian Americans were reading. From New York City came the daily *Il Progresso Italo-Americano*, editor Generoso Pope. Other publications in Italian that came to Trenton, I know from what was mailed to our house: we received *La Follia di New York*, published by Riccardo Cordiferro, pen name of Alessandro Sisca, a friend of my grandfather; we also received a magazine called *Il Carroccio*.

Many families turned for their daily local news to the *State Gazette*, a morning newspaper, or the *Trenton Evening Times*, an afternoon newspaper. None of the people we knew read the *Daily True American* or the *Labor News*. Since my grandfather was an employee of the *Trenton Evening Times*, he brought with him a copy of the *Times* when he came home from work. My father for many years bought the *New York Journal*.

Books in Italian could be had by writing to the Vanni Company or to *La Libreria Italiana*, both in New York City, or from sources in Philadelphia.

For books in Italian available locally there was access to small collections to be found in the Main Library on Academy Street or in the Trenton Library Branch located at the corner of Hamilton and Chestnut Avenues, directly opposite the then Trenton High School.

Records were not available from the Trenton Free Public Library to show when the collections were started. From the date slip on the inside back cover of each book one can learn when the book was first borrowed. In books both in the Main collection and in the Branch collection the earliest date was 1917.

What could be learned by counting cards in the library files was that, as one could expect, novels constituted the largest number of books in Italian. For example, at the Main Library there were cards for 320 novels, 215 books of non-fiction, 23 books of plays, 29 books of poetry. There were books by authors such as Vasari, Ariosto, D'Annunzio, Aristophanes, Boccaccio, Brocchi, Pearl Buck, Carducci, Montessori, Joseph Conrad, Dante, Deledda, Dumas, Fogazzaro, Franklin, Pirandello, Shakespeare, Tasso, Tolstoi, Verne, and Zola. In additon, there were cookery books, books on child care, religion, and there were dictionaries.

At the present Briggs Branch, which contains the books from the old branch library at Hamilton and Chestnut Avenues, there were roughly 210 books, including books by Deledda, Brocchi, D'Annunzio, Dante, Pirandello, and many others. There were translations of Crawford, Cervantes, Andersen and Wells. Crawford's *Corleone* had been borrowed 44 times from April 1924 to June 1956. Another popular book was Crawford's *Saracinesca* borrowed 44 times from June 1921 to December 1950. Jules Verne was also popular with 33 borrowings of his *Adventures of Three Russians and Three Englishmen in South Africa* from May 1922 to November 1971.

At the Briggs Branch there were 149 titles of novels, 46 of non-fiction, five of poetry, and five of plays.

Music was, and is, an important element in Italian culture. In 1907 the Mascagni Italian Band was incorporated. There were five other bands that readily come to mind when one thinks of the old days. One was conducted by Vito De Lorenzo, another by Frank S. Lanza, a third by Vincenzo Vosa, a fourth by Benedetto Napoliello, and the fifth was Colletti's Band. Lanza, Vosa, and Napoliello also taught music and various instruments.

There are two other areas to touch on briefly – motion pictures and radio. The Italian Americans were avid moviegoers. On occasion motion pictures in Italian were made available to a hungry public. For example, at the Park Theater, formerly the City Square, films such as *I Pagliacci* were shown. At the corner of Chestnut and Morris Avenues there was the Bella Theater – John Bella, Proprietor. Notices of films to be shown at the Bella Theater in English appeared regularly in the *Trenton Evening Times*. Occasionally films in Italian would be shown, such as, *Gli Ultimi Giorni di Pompei, I Figli di Nessuno* and *Quo Vadis*. As late as 1931 Hunt's State Theater ran an advertisement for the showing on Sunday only of the re-run of a film in Italian.[16] The advertisement ran as follows:

Ritorna a Trenton	Returns to Trenton
Un altro super-film	Another super-film

della	of the
Cines-Pittaluga	Cines-Pittaluga Studio
Corte D'Assise	"The Court of Assizes"
100% Parlata e Cantata	100% Spoken and Sung
in Italiano	in Italian
Con Titolo in Inglese	English Sub-Titles

There were many movie houses throughout the city that Italians frequented. In the Chambersburg area, for example, there were a number: on South Clinton Avenue near Chestnut Avenue there was the Bijou Theater; on South Broad Street at Hudson Street there was the Victory Theater; a few blocks farther south on Broad Street quite a large theater was built – the Broad Theater. Off Hamilton Avenue at the fork of Anderson and Washington Streets there was the City Square Theater, later called the Park Theater, and on Chestnut Avenue near Morris Avenue there was the Bella Theater, also known as the B B Theater. Some would go to the theaters in the center of the city. On East State Street there were the Stacy, the State, and the Orpheum theaters; on South Broad Street just off State Street there was the Capitol Theater, and on North Warren Street there was the Trent Theater, and much later just north of the Trent the Lincoln Theater was built.

Those who knew no English could enjoy and understand what they saw at these theaters. My grandmother was one of these. Although she spoke no English and could read only the Italian language, she could read easily enough the very highly emotive acting which characterized the silent films of those days. With the coming of the "talkies" in the late twenties, she could no longer derive the same pleasure from these films that the "silents" had always given her.

With the advent of radio, a source of entertaiment on a daily basis and in one's own home became available. This meant that Italian-speaking people could tune in to New York City and enjoy the skits, music, songs, and serial dramas in Italian that were being scheduled. In Trenton, radio became synonymous with the name Michael Fonde.

Mike, as he was called by all, was born on August 20, 1909, at Sliema, on the Island of Malta and he emigrated to the United States in 1929. His father had come here before World War I and settled in Morrisville, Pennsylvania, where he was a railroad worker. Mike's first work experience here was at the King Farm; from this he went to the rubber mill in Morrisville. In those days he played mandolin and became part of a trio of guitar, mandolin and accordion. He went to Station WTNJ, and helped the manager set things up at the Hotel Stacy-Trent, where WTNJ was to broadcast. He ran the controls so satisfactorily that he was hired and in 1934 was asked to produce an Italian program. This resulted in a weekly program, which then grew to a program broadcast five times a week, Monday through Friday; on Saturday mornings, he would broadcast recordings of complete operas. He then went to Station WTTM, where he broadcast another program while he continued with his WTNJ program. Filippo Neri then took over at WTNJ. After a few years the WTNJ program went to Antonio Vigliano.

At WTTM Fonde produced a live program on Thursday evenings entitled "Neapolitan Nights". Raffaele Volpe was the *macchiettista i.e.,* singer of humorous, satiric songs; Amadeo Dinzo was accordionist; Peter Rose guitarist; and Antonio Vella mandolinist. The program was sponsored by the Trenton Beverage Company, owned by Armando Conti.

Family Pastimes and Customs

This overview of Italian American life in Trenton will end with what individual families did for amusement. Since only two families are dealt with, this section cannot be taken to say that all Italian families did the same things or observed certain customs in the same way. The two families are from Naples and a nearby town: they are the Bilancios and the Ruffo-Ciccolellas.

It was from her grandfather that Rose Bilancio acquired the oral history and background of the Bilancios. In the main, as Mrs. Rose Bilancio recalls, the Bilancio family would rely on themselves, as virtually all families did, for their entertainment. As was quite customary, her father, Nicola, was the mainspring. He activated the discussions during their evening meal. She recalls that in good part the talk was of topics of the day. She remembers that the talk was especially animated when such matters as the death of Enrico Caruso, the incidents involving Arturo Giovanitti and Carlo Tresca, and the trial of Sacco and Vanzetti were of major concern to the Italians. Her father's role after dinner was no less important. Relatives and friends would drop in almost every evening; hence, they themselves did little visiting. The talk would turn again to the topics that had occupied them during dinner. Then there was singing – all in Italian – led by the father. The singing not only served to pass the time pleasantly; it would also act as a salve. Mrs. Bilancio remembers that minor frictions – among family members or with their neighbors – would be smoothed over by some of the singing sessions.

In summer the family would sit out on the sidewalk with neighbors and pass the time chatting. She remembers that on very hot nights at about eleven the older women in their usual black dresses would make use of the water spray from the fire hydrant to cool off a bit.

The women would involve the children when canning was to be done. They canned tomatoes, and the children would be part of the process. In many families the children were also involved in the making of *conserva*, what we call tomato paste. After the tomatoes had been passed through a sieve and drained, they would be spread out on boards in a thin layer to dry in the sun. I can still remember both the sight and the fragrance of this conserva as I would pass by the backyards of homes where this was done. Rose feels that these family activities cemented the bond of family even more strongly because all the family members sensed that they were all working together for the good of all. On summer Sunday afternoons, the Bilancio family walked on Hamilton Avenue or on Greenwood Avenue. Occasionally they would walk to Stacy Park or to the Pennsylvania Railroad Station to watch the people who were coming and going. At times there would be a family trip on the Delaware River by excursion boat to Burlington, where the family would have a picnic lunch before the ride back to Trenton.

Saturday evenings were usually devoted to going to one of the moving picture houses such as the Victory Theater or the Bijou Theater.

In winter there were the visits already mentioned. At that time of year the family engaged in such passive entertainment as listening to the father read novels aloud in Italian; he read one chapter a night so that a complete segment would be heard at each reading. She remembers his reading *Genoveffa* and *Il Conte di Monte Cristo*. Occasionally he would read articles to the family from the newspapers he bought: *Il Nuovo Mondo* (The New World) and *Il Progresso Italo-Americano*. It was during the winter months, too, that Mr. Bilancio and his father-in-law played games with the rest of the family. She remembers vividly some of the games they played to while away the long winter evenings. One was called "The Beetle", in which one person sat on the floor with his head near the knees of the other person playing the game who was seated and with his knees slightly apart. The trick was to avoid getting his head squeezed between the other's knees when they would suddenly be brought together. Other games played were "Sacco" – very much like our hide and go seek – and a game like marbles, but played with hazel nuts or filberts instead of marbles or taws. A very popular guessing game played by virtually all was "Morra". In this game for two players, both hands are used – the left hand as a fist is held down and a finger is extended each time the player guesses correctly. The guessing is done when, with the right hand, which is on call and extended with one, two, or whatever number of fingers showing, the player calls out the total number of fingers showing on the extended hands of the two players. The players decide in advance how many extensions will constitute a game – five to ten.

While some of these games were being played, the very young children were kept amused by their grandfather who would dandle each in turn on his knees all the while chanting rhymes in a sing-song.

Like the Bilancios many families engaged in activities of their own. Our family, for example, also had visitors coming in. The Raffaele Volpes and Sigismondo Fantauzzos came to visit every weekday evening. On Sunday evenings at eight o'clock Raffaele and Emilia Volpe came with their six children. The evenings were spent in conversation, the topics ranging from recollections of Naples, home town of my mother and of the Volpes, and of Casteltermini, Mr. Fantauzzo's home town, to politics, the Order Sons of Italy, Antonio Meucci and the telephone, my grandfather's experiences as a Bersagliere, etc. These weekday evenings were always topped off with a demi-tasse of Italian coffee.

On Sundays when the Volpes came, there would be singing by Mr. Volpe at the player piano operated by my father or there would be dancing by Mr.

and Mrs. Volpe. I first saw the tango danced when the Volpes entertained us one Sunday evening, and always there was conversation. On Sundays our guests were offered Italian coffee, *paste* (pastries or cookies), and *un bicchierino* (a small glass, which figuratively meant a liqueur). Invitations to dinner were exchanged with the Volpes and the Fantauzzos. These varied the otherwise unchanging routine of daily visits.

Because my grandfather was very active in the Order Sons of Italy we would attend affairs out of town, and at convention times we would all go with my grandfather to the state conventions. On occasion we would also attend national conventions held in places other than in New Jersey or New York; I remember attending conventions in Boston and in Norfolk.

The fact that we had relatives and friends in New York City and in Brooklyn accounted for our going with some frequency to New York. For my brother and me, these organizations and social trips out of town were of great educational value. I can still remember that it was on one of these trips that I was taken to the top of the Woolworth Building, then the world's tallest building. We – the Ciccolellas – used to spend the month of July in Brooklyn at my uncle's house. It was during those vacation days in the 1920s that I was taken to see Max Reinhardt's "The Miracle" with Lady Diana Manners. It was during another July that I saw the D'Oyly Carte Company's production of Gilbert and Sullivan's "Iolanthe". Another vivid recollection of mine is that of having gone to hear Rosa Ponselle sing at the Shriners Temple in Trenton; it was my first exposure to "live" operatic singing. This new interest culminated in my first visit to the Metropolitan Opera House in the 1930s to hear Verdi's "La Forza del Destino" conducted by Bruno Walter.

Families observed such special days as the Feast of St. Joseph, which falls on March 19. The Neapolitan observance features the eating of *zeppole*, ring-shaped dough fried in deep oil. The light, airy dough, after having been fried to a golden color is covered with yellow cream which is topped with pieces of candied fruits.

For the Sicilians, whose patron saint is St. Joseph, there is the setting of *la tavola di San Giuseppe*, the St. Joseph Table. According to research done by the Rev. Richard Amico of Batavia, New York, the custom of the St. Joseph Table has its origin in the middle ages. At a time when the island of Sicily was laid waste by an extremely severe drought, the feudal landowners turned to St. Joseph, the island's patron saint, for help. They made a vow that, if the rains came, they would prepare a lavish feast in his honor and invite all the people of the area. The rains came and, true to their word, the landowners did indeed prepare a big feast. They set up tables in the village square and invited all those who came to help themselves.

The practice from that time on spread, and now the feast is observed by congregational feasting at which the elderly needy are invited and given bread and vegetables from the St. Joseph Table, or by individuals who have made a vow to set such a table in their home if the favor prayed for has been granted.

Even today congregants of St. James R.C. Church meet on or about March 19 to attend a feast at which the St. Joseph Table is the attraction. The table is some 25 feet in length and spread with white cloth. On it at regular intervals are seven-pound loaves of bread made in a number of traditional shapes. Each shape represents something having to do with St. Joseph; it must be understood, of course, that these shapes are stylized rather than truly representational. There are, for example, loaves to suggest St. Joseph, his beard, the infant Jesus, St. Joseph's staff topped with blossoms, and a ring-shaped loaf to suggest the Blessed Virgin. At the center of the table but behind it on a raised stand or altar is placed a plaster statue of St. Joseph with his staff resting on his right arm and the infant Jesus on his left arm. At each end of the table are placed vases filled with fresh flowers. Over all the loaves and in the spaces between them are laid stalks of celery and the off-white bottoms of fresh fennel, heads of romaine lettuce, eggplants, heads of escarole, tomatoes, artichokes, and peppers. All along the table are strewn apples and oranges adding additional vivid colors to the various tints of green of the vegetables.

What has just been described is a communal observance, with those present partaking of a dinner. The St. Joseph bread is then cut and distributed among the diners; the fruits and vegetables are also distributed. All that has been distributed is to be taken home and given to others, preferably the elderly needy.

But the St. Joseph Table is also personal observance. Customarily it is set up in one's own house for prayers answered because of St. Joseph's intercession. This, of course, is, by comparison to the communal ritual, much smaller but no less colorful. The elderly needy are invited to dinner and the fruits and vegetables and bread are given to them to take home. This custom is followed by some Sicilians even today. I have learned that some Calabrians also set up such a table, but theirs honors St. Anthony.

There are customs which are practiced just before and during the Lenten season. As told me by Vito J. Brenna, on Mardi Gras, the Tuesday before Ash Wednesday, the end of the Carneval season which precedes the gray and Spartan Lent, the Sanfelesi relish a macaroni dish with red sauce on which has been sprinkled grated horseradish. Others, as was so with our family, prepared a dinner rich in pork. We usually had for first course gnocchi with a red, pork (mainly sausage) sauce. Then followed the sausage of the sauce and a roast of pork. The dessert — besides the customary fruit of the season — was *sanguinaccio*, a blood pudding made with sugar, milk, chocolate, butter, starch, vanilla, cinnamon, eggs, pieces of candied citron and pig's blood. The whole becomes a satiny smooth, extremely flavorful pudding.

A custom which now seems to have disappeared completely is the breaking of the *pignata*, a cooking pot made of terra cotta. After being filled with chocolate kisses, lollipops, hard candy, and tootsie rolls, it was decorated with gay bunting and suspended over an open space that would admit of wildly aimed blows delivered by blindfolded children. The contents just named were those used in our house. The terra cotta pot was used if available, but I remember that most of the time shoe boxes were the containers of the candies. My brother and I would be blindfolded, given three-foot long wooden rods or sticks, spun about several times, and told to strike at the suspended pignata until one of us broke it. Then we would gather the candies and enjoy them. The breaking of the pignata must have come into Italy with the Spanish Bourbons. How widely this was practiced in southern Italy I do not know. Since we observed this custom I know that it must have been common in Campania. It was observed in Campania on the first Sunday of Lent, perhaps as a reminder that the good, rich times of Carnevale had to give way to the penitential time of Lent. It must have also been enjoyed in Umbria and in Lazio because I was told by Dino Cattani that he remembers the custom in his native Terni.

For us at home Holy Week, the week before Easter, was filled with preparations for the Easter joy and the festive table that would be set. On Palm Sunday we – my mother, my father, my brother, my sister and I -would go to church, where we would receive the palms. After dinner we would sit around the dinner table and create ornate crosses made of the palms that we would wear pinned to our shirts for the rest of the day. There were other uses for the palms: one was to place part of the frond in the frame of the religious pictures that were in my mother's and in my grand-mother's bedrooms; another was to bunch a few fronds together to dip into a bowl of holy water which we would get from St. Joachim's Church. At the Easter dinner the bound palm fronds would be used to sprinkle holy water over the table and each of us as a blessing. This was done by the oldest member of the family, my grandfather.

During Holy Week we expected a visit from the pastor or one of the curates for the annual blessing of the house. Good Friday evening my mother, with my brother and me in tow, would make *la visita ai sepolcri* (the visit to the sepulchers). This meant that we would start at our parish church, which was just around the corner on Butler Street, and go to the Church of the Immaculate Conception on Chestnut Avenue. After we had bought a family automobile in 1934 and my brother and I could drive, we would visit two additional churches which were too far away to walk to. These might be the Church of the Blessed Sacrament, the Church of the Sacred Heart, St. Hedwig's Church, or the Church of St. Francis.

The morning and the afternoon of Good Friday were filled with work for my mother and my grandmother. It was then that the baking would be done. In the morning the *casatiello* was made and baked. For this we would buy two one-pound balls of bread dough at one of the nearby bakers. This would be kneaded with lard with had been rendered at home. From this rendering there would remain *ciccioli* (flavorful scraps of pork deep fried during the rendering). Part of these would be added to the dough along with a good bit of freshly ground black pepper. The kneaded dough would then be twisted into a ring. On the top would be placed six raw eggs, one for each member of the family, and these would be held in place by thin ropes of dough in the shape of a cross.

During the afternoon the *pastiera di grano* would be made. This is a very flavorful Neapolitan confection, one of whose ingredients is grains of wheat which had been softened by being soaked in water and then boiled in milk. Other ingredients are eggs, sugar, ricotta, pieces of fresh orange peel, candied citron, and as a flavoring agent *neroli* (essential oil of oranges) or orange blossom water. This last is of the utmost importance because it is the one element which imparts to the confection its special flavor. The ingredients are placed in a shell of sweet dough and the top is latticed. After the pastiera is removed from the oven and allowed to cool, confectioner's sugar is sprinkled over it.

A less expensive and less time-consuming pastiera is made with noodles or spaghetti, eggs, milk, vanilla (some also use cinnamon), and sugar. This too is baked and is quite flavorful.

The pastiera di grano is a specialty eaten only at Easter. My father, not a Neapolitan, also wanted pastiera for *la piccola pasqua* (the little Easter), that is, Pentecost.

On Easter the four of us would attend the solemn High Mass at St. Mary's Cathedral. The mid-afternoon dinner was preceded by the blessing already mentioned. The dinner itself opened with a vegetable soup, made only for the Easter dinner, consisting of beef stock, tiny meatballs, escarole, and *cicoria* (radicchio or chicory). Then there would be lasagne or baked ziti, followed by either lamb or roast kid when available; for variety the lamb was also served as *spezzatino* – sauted in butter and egg yolk, and flavored with fresh lemon, oregano, parsley, and garlic. Always as part of the Easter dinner, the casatiello was eaten with two or three types of sausages: *soppressata* (a type of salame); Genoa salame; what is today called pepperoni; and links of dried sausage flavored with coarsely ground black pepper.

The salad was always cicoria with the usual dressing of olive oil and wine vinegar. Fruit would follow, and the climax came with the pastiera and Italian coffee to close the dinner.

When I was a boy in the mid-twenties, Italian roast coffee was not available in Trenton. We used to go to Heroy's Tea Store at 23 E. Hanover Street but the best that could be had there was French roast coffee. We took to buying the coffee beans and roasting them at home. This was my chore. The roaster was the size and shape of a skillet with a lid which had a sliding vent in it; its handle was wooden and some two feet long. I would pour the coffee beans into the roaster and hold it over the burner of the gas stove we had in a shed behind the kitchen, all the while keeping the beans moving to assure that all were being evenly roasted. There would be a good deal of smoke coming from the roaster which carried the pungent, pleasant aroma of the coffee around the area. When the beans had turned black and had a sheen from the oil in them, I knew that they had been properly roasted. The beans were then spread out and allowed to cool. My next chore was to use the coffee mill, adjust it to give the proper grind, and set to work.

In addition to the religious festivals, there were family picnics, trips to visit friends and relatives, and occasional trips to points on the Jersey shore to help us pass the summer months. The observance of some traditional days did not require time off from work. One holy day – August 15, the day of the Assumption – and a national holiday – Ferragosto, in Italy – could be celebrated simply by buying and eating a watermelon, a custom still practiced in Naples.

Thanksgiving Day, a typically American holiday, was observed at home, but it was not until many years later that we ate turkey with the customary fixings. At home we had capon, which my grandfather preferred, preceded, as one would expect, by lasagne. The holiday was not referred to as Thanksgiving Day but as *la festa delle gallinc* (the chicken holiday).

The year culminated with Christmas. My brother Angelo and I did not know of Santa Claus until we enrolled in the Centennial School, when we were initiated into the pre-Christmas rites of the singing of carols, and of working at crayon drawings of Christmas trees, holly, and – of course – Santa Claus. For us there was *La Befana* (a corruption of the Italian *epifania*, epiphany), the mythical figure of an old woman who passes by earth from January 1 to January 6, the day of the Epiphany. On this last day the world was full of such prodigious happenings as trees bearing fruit, animals speaking, waters of rivers turning to gold. It was on this day too that children would await presents brought by La Befana.

Two years later, after having been introduced to Santa and having forsaken La Befana, we began to prepare for Christmas much earlier than ever before, on the Friday immediately following Thanksgiving. This change came about because a year or two after we bought a house on Bayard Street my grandfather decided that he wanted our Christmas celebration to include a *presepio*, Italian for the creche or manger. This meant much more, however, than the usual small group of Mary, Joseph, the infant Jesus, and the three Magi.

What he had in mind was a traditional Neapolitan display which relegated the nativity scene to what might be only an incidental part of the whole, which seemed to be rather a humanistic celebration of life among the ordinary people of Campania. In order to do this he needed to have enough room and he needed the figurines that any Neapolitan presepio demanded because of Neapolitan tradition and extravagance. The first requirement was met when the house was bought. The house had a living room or front room followed by another room. It was this second room that could be used to hold the presepio. The other requirement – the figurines – was met by my grandfather's writing to his brother in Santa Maria Capua Vetere, a few miles from Naples. His brother sent a full set in a strong wooden crate, each figurine carefully wrapped in cotton batting. However, because this was 1921, the crate had been thoroughly and roughly inspected for bottles of liquor at customs; as a result, none of the figurines had remained whole. We spent two full weeks gluing heads, arms and legs to torsos. These beautifully made and painted terra cotta figurines represented the countrymen and countrywomen of Campania of the early 1800s. They were shown at their varied occupations as they went about their daily lives.

My grandfather followed the traditional pattern. On saw horses he laid one-inch boards eight feet long to make a table eight feet long and five feet wide. This was the base upon which he built a frame for what was to be a mountain. The frame was stuffed with balls of crumpled newspaper. Brown wrapping paper was coated with paste and pressed upon the newspaper and shaped to simulate a rocky eminence. This was allowed to dry and then painted with water-soluble earth colors. Into the side of the mountain and about two feet above the base a recess had been fashioned to hold the manger, the Holy Family, and the cow and the donkey.

The figurines were spread about – people seemingly going about their affairs on an Italian mountainside which held, incongruously, the manger at Bethlehem. All in all it took about a month of working after dinner – after a day's work. The effort and time seemed to have been well spent because my grandfather derived great pleasure from what he had done. Friends and neighbors who came to visit or just to see the presepio were lavish with their praises, in which Grandpa basked.

In the front room the Christmas tree would be put up and trimmed the night of December 23. This was my father's task.

The morning and afternoon of Christmas Eve would be taken up by cooking and baking. As Easter would not be Easter without il casatiello and la pastiera, Christmas would not be Christmas without *gli struffoli* and other Christmas pastries. The struffoli are made from ropes of a simple egg dough cut into pieces about three-quarters of an inch long, deep fried in oil, then covered with honey, pieces of candied citron, and decorated with varicolored tiny jimmies. My mother also made a *tortano*, a ring of sweet dough filled with raisins and baked. We bought professionally-made pastries from Pasquale Landolfi. These were *roccocó*, a flat ring-shaped pastry flavored with roasted almonds; *susamielli*, an s-shaped sweet dough pastry flavored with almonds; and *mustacciuoli*, a diamond-shaped pastry also made of sweet dough and flavored with almonds. Some of these were also coated with chocolate.

The Christmas Eve dinner was, as was customary, meatless. We always opened the dinner with linguine in a red clam sauce. This was followed by escarole stuffed with anchovy, cut Sicilian black olives, capers, oregano, and bits of garlic; this was sprinkled with olive oil tied with string, and baked. Then there came fried squid, filet of sole, and fried *capitone*, a large type of eel. This capitone would be bought live two or three days before and kept in a tub of water until it was to be killed, skinned, and fried. I must confess that I did not find this very appealing. I did, however, enjoy the pickled eel that our dear friend Sigismondo Fantauzzo would make and bring to us in jars. And for my grandfather there was always a salad of boiled *baccalà* or dried codfish which was served with garlic, parsley, olive oil, and lemon juice. We always had an *insalata rinforza*, a salad made of pickled sweet red and green peppers, pickled vegetables such as onions, beans, cauliflowers, green and black olives, and anchovies. The whole was sprinkled with olive oil. Fruits, nuts, sun-dried figs or figs stuffed with almonds, baked, covered with a bay leaf, and packed in special wooden containers topped off the meal. For fruit we had tangerines, oranges, and apples.

At about 11:15 my brother and I would begin making preparations for a midnight ritual that included the young daughter, Lizzie, and the young son, Louie, of our *comare* Angelina De Simone, who had been widowed during the dread 1918 Spanish influenza epidemic and who spent all holidays at our house with her children.

My brother and I would go into the kitchen, where there was the coal stove, on and in which all cooking and baking was done. We would get the large imported pine cone and place it on the hot stove. Within minutes its fragrance would begin to rise and make its way to the dining room and beyond. As the pine cone, which was about five inches high and about four and a half inches in diameter at its widest point, began to react to the heat of the stove, its segments would curl out and reveal the *pignoli*, the pine nuts, which would then be shaken out to be eaten later. After all the segments had opened, we would turn the pine cone over so that the segments which were at the bottom and opened out made a concave area. During the afternoon, I would have already made with wire a contraption that would hold the upside-down pine cone so that it could be used as a censer. We would then place the pine cone in the contraption, place a red ember from the coal stove in it, and sprinkle incense which we had obtained from St. Joachim's on the ember.

My brother Angelo, Lizzie, Louie, and I would line up with Lizzie leading. She was the one who carried the figurine of the infant Jesus; Louie came next and sang the traditional Italian carol "Gesú Bambino"; Angelo carried the censer, and I came last with additional incense. At midnight we would march to the presepio. Lizzie would place the infant Jesus in the manger, Louie would go on singing several stanzas of the carol, Angelo would keep the censer moving slightly so that incense smoke would rise in gentle coils and spirals, and I stood ready to drop more incense into the censer as our little ceremony would be played out.

All of this might take five or six minutes. After warm exchanges of *Buon Natale*, Merry Christmas, we would all repair to the dining room for the midnight supper. The main item was the cutting and eating of a large *pizza rustica* – literally, a rustic pie – the ingredients of which are ricotta, mozzarella, pieces of provolone, bits of prosciutto and salame, eggs, freshly ground black pepper, all put in a deep pie crust made with shortening and baked. Insalata rinforza, various cheeses, nuts, tortano, and struffoli made up the supper.

Christmas was not remarkable in any way, except that along with the tortano and struffoli we had a tray of Neapolitan Christmas pastries made by Pasquale Landolfi.

After the long, late afternoon Christmas Dinner, dishes would be cleared away and washed. In the evening the time was spent playing *tombola*, what we call lotto or bingo. For markers we used dried beans, and we played for high stakes – pennies and nickels. The caller was my grandfather, who could call the numbers in the Italian fashion. He would draw a number and announce it by words or expressions which all the adults understood. For example, if he had drawn a four, he would call it *il porco* – for "the pig." Because the children did not know all the terms, he would then add "quattro", "four". The terms used vary from town to town. But those from the Naples area that come to mind are #1 – *l'Italia;* #4 – *il porco*, the pig; #6 – *il fesso*, the fool; #13 – *Sant' Antonio;* #17 – *la disgrazia*, the misfortune; #8 – *lo zoppo*, the lame man; #48 – *il morto che parla*, the talking dead man; and #90 – *la paura*, fear.

For New Year's Eve my aunt and uncle, their three daughters, and my spinster aunt would come from Brooklyn for a two-day visit. In addition to these six we would have all our close friends, some 35 persons, in for the New Year's party. Things would start moving at about 10 o'clock, when the Volpe family would arrive. Then the two Conte families would come, and a bit later the De Simones, the Fantauzzos, and some of my grandfather's friends from the *Trenton Times*. At 11:45 two large trays of pastries would be delivered by Mr. Landolfi. These were the usual *sfogliatelle, cannoli, napoleons, pasticciotti*, and *babbá a rum*. At midnight my grandfather went to the pile of pots, lids, and wooden ladles or sticks which were to be used at midnight, when we would go outside and bang away for five or six minutes. Then it was back inside where Italian coffee and liqueurs had been poured out to be consumed along with the delicious Landolfi confections.

For us the Christmas season ended with the day of the Epiphany, January 6. The next day saw the dismantling of the presepio. All the figurines would be gently wrapped in cotton batting and put away for their next appearance.

For some six years – that is, until 1926 – the presepio was part of our Christmas festivities. Then my grandfather was unable to work at it because his arthritis had worsened. My brother and I had reached an age when little processions were felt to be beneath our dignity, and so those practices succumbed to the passing of time. But the Christmas eve dinner, the Christmas night tombola, and the New Year's celebration continued for many years. Now only vestiges remain.

Appendix - Photos

Courtesy of Helen Del Monte and Nicholas S. D'Angelo

Officers of the St. John Italian Baptist Church posed with their pastor, circa 1921. They are, from left to right, front row: Mary Quallis, Lucy Petti, the Rev. Michael Solimene, Anna Gage Solimene, Anna Cardacino; second row: Luigi Martino, Orazio Previtera, Benedetto Cianfanco, Francesco Bonelli, Gerard Quallis; third row: Samuel Cardacino, Zopito Di Quinzio, Joseph Petti, Vito Del Monte.

The Centennial School, where the Roman Hall now stands.

Courtesy of the Trenton Free Public Library

Feast of St. Anthony, June 26-27, 1926 on Butler Street

Courtesy of John Conte

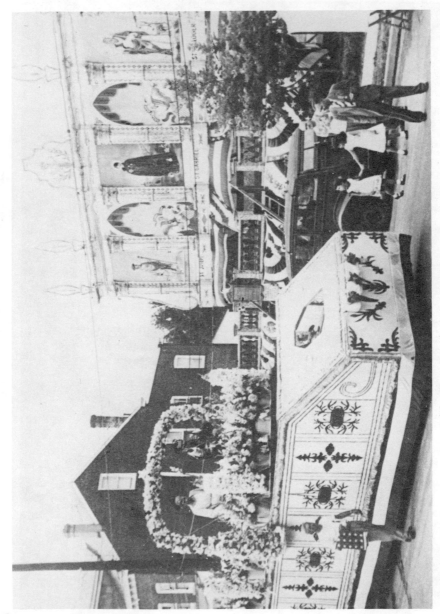

Celebration of St. Joseph and St. Calogero on E. Paul Avenue

Courtesy of Michael Schifano

Joseph Brenna in the Brenna brothers' grocery at 580 S. Clinton Avenue. 1910.

Courtesy of Vito J. Brenna

Courtesy of Lena Lo Bue Ballner

Alfonso Zarbo, left, with his employer Paul Schevitz, at 23 W. Hanover Street. 1915

Feast of St. Anthony on E. Paul Avenue.

Courtesy of Michael Schifano

Courtesy of Anthony Pacera

The 15th anniversary of the Casteltermini Mutual Aid Society, May 12, 1936. Old and new officers, from left, front row: Emanuel Butera, Joseph Pacera, Vincent Giuliano, Carmelo Severino, Carmen Caltagirone, Vincent Butera, Nicola Sciarrotta; second row: Joseph Russo, Frank Cellini, Gaetano Liuzzi, Joseph Plumeri, John Benedetti, Joseph Vitellaro; third row: Pietro Lo Curto, Calogero Midulla, Joseph Mulé, Salvatore Minuteli, Joseph Milioto;fourth row: Joseph Sciarrotta, Antonio Grigoli, Vincenzo Mangione, Frank Chimera, Menno Varsalona.

The front page of Il Secolo XX of May 3, 1923.

Courtesy of the Trenton Free Public Library

The placard held center is barely legible in the original photograph. It reads: "North Trenton Italians' Group Cheering the Victory and Italian Empire Declaration VV Il Duce (Long Live the Duce)". May 1936.

References

They Established Churches

[1] Item number 232 in Inventory of the Church Archives of New Jersey, Prepared by The Historical Records Survey, Division of Women's and Professional Projects, Works Progress Administration. Baptist Bodies. Newark, NJ. December 1938.

[2] From the incorporation records kept in the County Clerk's Office, Mercer County Court House, South Broad Street, Trenton, NJ.

[3] *Ibid.*

[4] *Ibid.*

[5] *Ibid.*

[6] Merzbacher, John S. *Trenton's Foreign Colonies.* Trenton, NJ. 1908. Chapter 4, page 96.

The Organizations They Founded

[1] Tocqueville, Alexis de. *Democracy in America.* New York: Alfred A. Knopf. 1960. page 191.

[2] These may be found in the New Jersey State Archives, in the State House Complex.

[3] Prezzolini, Giuseppe. *I Trapiantati.* Longanesl & Co. Milano. 1963. page 88.

[4] Bichelli, Pirro. *Grammatica del Dialetto Napoletano.* Edizione "Pegaso", Bari. 1973. page 9.

[5] *Enciclopedia Italiana.* Edizione 1949. Vol. VII. page 633.

[6] *Ibid.* Vol. V. page 840.

[7] *Ibid.* Vol. IX. page 557.

[8] Croce, Benedetto. *Storia D'Italia dal 1871 al 1915.* 1929. page 15.

[9] *Ibid.* page 39.

[10] *Enciclopedia Italiana.* Vol. XII. page 322.

[11] Signorelli, Pietro. *Storia D'Italia.* 1924. page 437.

[12] *The Columbia Encyclopedia.* Third Ed. 1956. page 366.

[13] *Ibid.* page 2168.

[14] Prezzolini. *Op. Cit.* page 89.

[15] *Enciclopedia Italiana.* Vol. V. page 54.

[16] Rasulo, Emilio. *Storia di Grumo, Frattamaggiore e I Suoi Uomini Illustri,* 1967. page 41.

[17] *Ibid.* page 41.

[18] *Ibid.* page 41.

[19] *Ibid.* page 61.

[20] *Ibid.* page 66.

Their Varied Activities

[1] *Trenton Times* September 3, 1900 p 1

[2] *Trenton Times* September 20, 1900 p 3

[3] *Trenton Times* September 24, 1900 p 1

[4] *Daily True American* September 15, 1901 p 5

[5] *Daily True American* September 16, 1901 p 5

[6] *Enciclopedia Italiana.* Edizione 1949. Roma. 1949. Vol. VI. p 778. The Bersaglieri were members of a special branch of the Italian Army's Infantry. It was created on June 18, 1836 to protect the line by rifle fire, by sharpshooting, and by firing while running.

[7] *Trenton Times* July 16, 1904 p 1

[8] *Trenton Times* September 20, 1900 p 1

[9] *Trenton Times* October 10, 1900 p 1

[10] *Trenton Times* January 8, 1902 p 1

[11] *Trenton Times* January 22, 1902 p 1

[12] *Daily True American* July 17, 1901 p 5

[13] *Trenton Times* July 16, 1902 p 1

[14] *Trenton Times* July 14, 1906 p 1

[15] *Trenton Times* September 5, 1907 p 1

[16] *Trenton Evening Times* September 10, 1921 p 3

[17] *Trenton Evening Times* September 8, 1911 p 11

[18] *Trenton Evening Times* September 14, 1911 p 2

[19] *Trenton Evening Times* January 24, 1919 p 9

[20] Minutes of the Trenton Board of Education for meeting of March 6, 1919

[21] Richard D. La Guardia, brother of New York City Mayor Fiorello La Guardia, was the industrial secretary of the Y.M.C.A., educational and welfare director at the N.J. State Prison in Trenton, editor of several newspapers in Trenton, and active in many civic affairs.

[22] *Sunday Times-Advertiser* September 1, 1935 p 5

[23] *Trenton Evening Times* March 15, 1939 p 4

[24] *Trenton Evening Times* March 21, 1939 p 16

[25] *Trenton Evening Times* October 6, 1939 p 3

[26] *Trenton Evening Times* November 4, 1930 p 4

[27] *Trenton Evening Times* July 13, 1932 p 3

[28] *Trenton Evening Times* January 31, 1934 p 3

[29] *Trenton Evening Times* February 10, 1934 p 5

[30] *Trenton Evening Times* May 24, 1935 p 4

[31] *Trenton Evening Times* May 31, 1935 p 3

[32] *Trenton Evening Times* February 11, 1936 p 2

[33] *Trenton Evening Times* February 27, 1936 p 2

34 *Trenton Evening Times* January 26, 1939 p 26

35 *Trenton Evening Times* June 1, 1936 p 3

36 *Trenton Evening Times* September 23, 1936 p 22

37 *Trenton Evening Times* September 30, 1936 p 3

38 *Trenton Evening Times* October 12, 1936 p 2

39 *Trenton Evening Times* February 8, 1937 p 22

40 *Trenton Evening Times* February 11, 1937 p 3

41 *Trenton Evening Times* October 1, 1937 p 4

42 *Trenton Evening Times* November 21, 1938 p 12

43 *Trenton Evening Times* March 22, 1939 p 5

44 *Trenton Evening Times* January 9, 1940 p 3

45 *Trenton Evening Times* January 31, 1940 p 8

46 *Trenton Evening Times* March 15, 1940 p 15

47 *Trenton Evening Times* June 19, 1940 p 18

48 *Trenton Evening Times* August 9, 1940 p 15

49 *Trenton Evening Times* September 20, 1940 p 32

50 *Trenton Evening Times* January 17, 1941 p 22

51 *Trenton Evening Times* April 15, 1941 p 14

52 *Trenton Evening Times* April 21, 1941 p 10

53 *Trenton Evening Times* April 25, 1941 p 17

54 *Trenton Evening Times* May 16, 1941 p 1

55 *Trenton Evening Times* June 13, 1941 p 17

56 *Trenton Evening Times* June 20, 1941 p 22

57 *Trenton Evening Times* August 1, 1941 p 6

58 *Trenton Evening Times* September 26, 1941 p 11

59 *Trenton Evening Times* March 6, 1942 p 19

60 *Trenton Evening Times* August 11, 1942 p 19

Americanization

1 *Trenton Evening Times* October 21, 1914 p 12

2 *Trenton Evening Times* October 14, 1921 p 3

2 *Trenton Evening Times* January 11, 1936 p 3

4 *Trenton Evening Times* March 31, 1939 p 2

5 *Trenton Evening Times* March 28, 1941 p 6

6 *Trenton Evening Times* November 27, 1941 p 28

7 *Trenton Evening Times* October 30, 1942 p 7

8 *Trenton Evening Times* November 4, 1942 p 16

In Political Activities

1 *Trenton Evening Times* November 1, 1915 p 4 Adv.

2 *State Gazette November 3, 1915 p 14*

3 *Trenton Evening Times* June 20, 1919 p 10

4 *Trenton Evening Times* October 28, 1919 p 10

5 *Trenton Evening Times* May 4, 1923 p 22 Adv.

6 *Il Secolo XX* May 3, 1923 p 1

7 *Trenton Evening Times* November 5, 1923 p 5

8 *Trenton Evening Times* October 15, 1926 p 1

9 *Trenton Evening Times* March 30, 1927 p 1

10 *Trenton Evening Times* April 22, 1927 p 35

11 *Trenton Evening Times* June 13, 1930 p 3

12 *Trenton Evening Times* January 10, 1936 p 14

13 *Trenton Evening Times* February 5, 1936 p 18

14 *Trenton Evening Times* March 5, 1936 p 4

15 *Trenton Evening Times* May 12, 1936 p 2

16 *Trenton Evening Times* June 25, 1936 p 11

17 *Trenton Evening Times* January 4, 1937 p 3

18 *Trenton Evening Times* February 24, 1937 p 5

19 *Trenton Evening Times* September 27, 1937 p 3

20 *Trenton Evening Times* March 29, 1938 p 6

21 *Trenton Evening Times* May 23, 1938 p 3

22 *Trenton Evening Times* March 29, 1940 p 5

23 *Trenton Evening Times* August 14, 1942 p 4

Education: One of Their Concerns

1 *Trenton Times* August 15, 1905 p 1

2 *Trenton Evening Times* March 8, 1918 p 10

3 *Trenton Evening Times* January 7, 1919 p 9

4 *Trenton Evening Times* January 10, 1919 p 11

5 *Trenton Evening Times* March 17, 1919 p 10

6 *Trenton Evening Times* October 30, 1919 p 18

7 *Trenton Evening Times* April 9, 1920 p 18

8 *Trenton Evening Times* March 2, 1929 p 14

9 *Trenton Evening Times* June 6, 1930 p 2

10 *Trenton Evening Times* June 6, 1930 p 2

[11] *Trenton Evening Times* June 13, 1930 p 28

[12] *Trenton Evening Times* June 16, 1930 p 4

[13] *Trenton Evening Times* June 10, 1930 p 20

[14] *Trenton Evening Times* January 26, 1934 p 9

[15] *Trenton Evening Times* May 29, 1935 p 4

[16] *Trenton Evening Times* June 1, 1935 p 7

[17] *Trenton Evening Times* June 22, 1936 P 3

[18] *Trenton Evening Times* June 26, 1936 p 4

[19] *Trenton Evening Times* October 1, 1937 p 4

War Times

[1] *Trenton Evening Times* February 27, 1918 p 11

[2] *Trenton Evening Times* January 7, 1919 p 3

[3] *Trenton Evening Times* January 15, 1919 p 14

[4] *Trenton Evening Times* November 12, 1919 p 12

[5] *Trenton Evening Times* November 15, 1919 p 1

[6] *Trenton Evening Times* November 17, 1919 p 10

[7] *Trenton Evening Times* February 20, 1936 p 3

[8] *Sunday Times-Advertiser* March 15, 1936 p 10 Part I

[9] *Trenton Evening Times* June 8, 1936 p 1

[10] *Trenton Evening Times* November 20, 1940 p 11

[11] *Trenton Evening Times* January 8, 1941 p 5

[12] *Trenton Evening Times* September 15, 1941 p 14

[13] *Trenton Evening Times* November 14, 1941 p 36

[14] *Trenton Evening Times* November 25, 1941 p 7

[15] *Trenton Evening Times* December 5, 1941 p 20

[16] *Trenton Evening Times* December 15, 1941 p 1

[17] *Trenton Evening Times* December 19, 1941 p 19

[18] *Trenton Evening Times* December 19, 1941 p 28

[19] *Trenton Evening Times* December 19, 1941 p 28

[20] *Trenton Evening Times* December 23, 1941 p 12

[21] *Trenton Evening Times* December 29, 1941 p 5

[22] *Trenton Evening Times* December 30, 1941 p 12

[23] *Trenton Evening Times* January 14, 1942 p 4

[24] *Trenton Evening Times* January 29, 1942 p 24

[25] *Trenton Evening Times* February 2, 1942 p 8

[26] *Trenton Evening Times* February 4, 1942 p 14

[27] *Trenton Evening Times* February 4, 1942 p 14

[28] *Trenton Evening Times* February 19, 1942 p 24

[29] *Trenton Evening Times* April 24, 1942 p 9

[30] *Trenton Evening Times* May 22, 1942 p 6

[31] *Trenton Evening Times* July 17, 1942 p 4

[32] *Trenton Evening Times* October 7, 1942 p 4

[33] *Trenton Evening Times* December 2, 1942 p 12

[34] *Trenton Evening Times* December 29, 1942 p 4

Club Dinners and Banquets

[1] *Trenton Evening Times* September 14, 1911 p 2

[2] *Trenton Evening Times* November 15, 1919 p 1

[3] *Trenton Evening Times* October 13, 1921 p 19

[4] *Trenton Evening Times* October 13, 1921 p 7

[5] *Trenton Evening Times* June 26, 1935 p 9

[6] *Trenton Evening Times* February 7, 1936 p 24

[7] *Trenton Evening Times* May 12, 1936 p 2

[8] *Trenton Evening Times* February 11, 1937 p 3

[9] *Trenton Evening Times* February 5, 1937 p 10

[10] *Trenton Evening Times* September 13, 1937 p 3

[11] *Trenton Evening Times* October 12, 1937 p 3

[12] *Trenton Evening Times* October 20, 1937 p 13

[13] *Trenton Evening Times* November 17, 1937 p 20

[14] *Trenton Evening Times* March 11, 1938 p 7

[15] *Trenton Evening Times* May 12, 1938 p 8

[16] *Trenton Evening Times* June 16, 1938 p 2

[17] *Trenton Evening Times* January 24, 1940 p 16

[18] *Trenton Evening Times* May 8, 1940 p 3

[19] *Trenton Evening Times* August 23, 1940 p 5

[20] *Trenton Evening Times* December 6, 1940 p 17

[21] *Trenton Evening Times* January 23, 1941 p 14

[22] *Trenton Evening Times* February 21, 1941 p 3

[23] *Trenton Evening Times* February 26, 1941 p 3

[24] *Trenton Evening Times* April 24, 1941 p 26

[25] *Trenton Evening Times* October 31, 1941 p 18

[26] *Trenton Evening Times* January 22, 1942 p 4

[27] *Trenton Evening Times* February 13, 1942 p 18

[28] *Trenton Evening Times* February 13, 1942 p 24

[29] *Trenton Evening Times* April 10, 1942 p 4

[30] *Trenton Evening Times* April 17, 1942 p 12

[31] *Trenton Evening Times* August 28, 1942 p 18

[32] *Trenton Evening Times* November 12, 1942 p 9

[33] *Trenton Evening Times* November 19, 1942 p 13

[34] *Trenton Evening Times* November 20, 1942 p 4

Just for Fun

[1] *Trenton Evening Times* October 29, 1931 p 21

[2] *Trenton Evening Times* November 10, 1931 p 14

[3] *Trenton Evening Times* January 3, 1935 p 20

[4] *Trenton Evening Times* January 18, 1935 p 14

[5] *Trenton Evening Times* May 31, 1935 p 3

[6] *Trenton Evening Times* January 30, 1936 p 32

[7] *Trenton Evening Times* February 20, 1936 p 9

[8] *Trenton Evening Times* June 25, 1936 p 11

[9] *Trenton Evening Times* May 11, 1937 p 7

[10] *Trenton Evening Times* November 17, 1937 p 20

[11] *Trenton Evening Times* April 26, 1938 p 7

[12] *Trenton Evening Times* May 26, 1938 p 15

[13] *Trenton Evening Times* June 14, 1938 p 18

[14] *Trenton Evening Times* November 16, 1938 p 9

[15] *Trenton Evening Times* November 28, 1939 p 4

[16] *Trenton Evening Times* January 31, 1941 p 24

[17] *Trenton Evening Times* February 12, 1941 p 10

[18] *Trenton Evening Times* February 26, 1941 p 3

[19] *Trenton Evening Times* May 27, 1941 p 13

[20] *Trenton Evening Times* July 8, 1941 p 7

[21] *Trenton Evening Times* November 13, 1941 p 13

[22] *Trenton Evening Times* December 17, 1941 p 20

[23] *Trenton Evening Times* February 13, 1942 p 18

[24] *Trenton Evening Times* June 21, 1939 p 3

In the News

[1] *Trenton Evening Times* July 16, 1904 p 10

[2] *Trenton Evening Times* August 15, 1905 p 9

[3] *Trenton Evening Times* February 26, 1918 p 11

[4] *Trenton Evening Times* January 3, 1919 p 15

[5] *Trenton Evening Times* January 24, 1919 p 11

[6] *Trenton Evening Times* October 15, 1919 p 18

[7] *Trenton Evening Times* November 1, 1919 p 14

[8] *Trenton Evening Times* August 2, 1911 p 7

[9] *Trenton Evening Times* November 19, 1919 p 12

[10] *Trenton Evening Times* February 23, 1923 p 17

[11] *Trenton Evening Times* September 21, 1926 p 15

[12] *Trenton Evening Times* March 1, 1929 p 4

[13] *Trenton Evening Times* November 3, 1931 p 8

[14] *Trenton Evening Times* November 12, 1931 p 9

[15] *Trenton Evening Times* January 17, 1934 p 16

[16] *Trenton Evening Times* February 1, 1937 p 5

[17] *Trenton Evening Times* February 23, 1937 p 1

[18] *Trenton Evening Times* August 3, 1938 p 3

[19] *Trenton Evening Times* August 12, 1938 p 8

[20] *Trenton Evening Times* August 18, 1938 p 5

[21] *Trenton Evening Times* November 9, 1938 p 15

[22] *Trenton Evening Times* November 11, 1938 p 11

[23] *Trenton Evening Times* September 5, 1939 p 3

[24] *Trenton Evening Times* October 5, 1939 p 3

[25] *Trenton Evening Times* October 31, 1939 p 7

[26] *Trenton Evening Times* November 1, 1939 p 3

[27] *Trenton Evening Times* November 3, 1939 p 24

[28] *Trenton Evening Times* December 26, 1939 p 12

[29] *Trenton Evening Times* January 25, 1940 p 11

[30] *Trenton Evening Times* February 14, 1940 p 9

[31] *Trenton Evening Times* February 21, 1940 p 7

[32] *Trenton Evening Times* April 3, 1940 p 2

[33] *Trenton Evening Times* July 19, 1940 p 3

[34] *Trenton Evening Times* October 17, 1940 p 9

[35] *Trenton Evening Times* December 5, 1940 p 13

[36] *Trenton Evening Times* December 20, 1940 p 22

[37] *Trenton Evening Times* January 10, 1941 p 22

[38] *Trenton Evening Times* March 17, 1941 p 12

[39] *Trenton Evening Times* May 2, 1941 p 18

[40] *Trenton Evening Times* July 24, 1941 p 4

[41] *Trenton Evening Times* September 18, 1941 p 15

[42] *Trenton Evening Times* September 22, 1941 p 5

[43] *Trenton Evening Times* October 16, 1941 p 30

[44] *Trenton Evening Times* December 5, 1941 p 5

[45] *Trenton Evening Times* May 19, 1942 p 16

[46] *Trenton Evening Times* June 10, 1942 p 16

[47] *Trenton Evening Times* June 16, 1942 p 16

[48] *Trenton Evening Times* July 23, 1942 p 22

[49] *Trenton Evening Times* October 26, 1942 p 7

Other Cultural Activities

[1] *Trenton Evening Times* May 24, 1935 p 4

[2] *Trenton Evening Times* February 27, 1942 p 24

[3] *Trenton Evening Times* March 25, 1940 p 7

[4] *Trenton Evening Times* October 23, 1940 p 12

[5] *Trenton Evening Times* March 15, 1939 p 4

[6] *Trenton Evening Times* April 9, 1938 p 7

[7] *Trenton Evening Times* June 18, 1910 p 2

[8] *Trenton Evening Times* September 16, 1938 p 8

[9] *Trenton Evening Times* April 19, 1940 p 23

[10] *Trenton Evening Times* November 10, 1936 p 4

[11] *Sunday Times-Advertiser* March 15, 1936 p 10 Part I

[12] *Trenton Evening Times* September 14, 1921 p 3

[13] *Trenton Evening Times* December 24, 1930 p 2

[14] *Labor News* May 5, 1938 p 5

[15] Names and dates found in the City Directories of Trenton from 1905 to the 1930s.

[16] *Trenton Evening Times* November 7, 1931 p 8

Index

INDEX

INDEX

INDEX

INDEX

INDEX

INDEX

INDEX

INDEX

Rizzo, Vitantonio, 24
Robbins School, 70-73
Roberto Bracco Dramatic Club, 39
Rochester, New York, 32
Rochester, New York, 9
Roda, Anthony, 44
Rodenwald, William, 63
Roebling Avenue Democratic Club, 57
Roebling's, 19, 77, 93
Rofi, Amedeo, 46
Roma Civic League of Trenton, N.J., 60, 67
Roma Building and Loan Association, 21
Roman Beneficial Society, 41, 64, 75
Roman Social Club of Chambersburg, 65
Roman Social Club, 58
Roman Society, 113
Roman Women's Mutual Aid Society, 40
Romani, Julius, 52
Romano, Frank, 112, 116
Rome, 1, 37, 75, 76
Romeo, Charles J., 101
Ronca, 130
Ronca, Cesare, 47, 111
Ronca, Davide C., 64
Ronca, Felice, 111
Ronzoni Program Company, 73
Roosevelt, President, 108
Rosalbino, Ammirato, 47
Rosario, Amico, 53
Rosati, Antonio, 41
Rose, Peter, 133
Rosemont Social Club, 40, 61
Ross, Antonio, 41

Rossi's B.B. Team, 68
Rossi, Ada, 54
Rossi, Armando, R., 29
Rossi, Bartolino, 48
Rossi, Lorenzo, 48
Rossi, Morris, 52
Rotunda, Frank, 116
Rotunno, Luigi, 41
Rubino, Saturday, 100
Ruffo, Angelo, 1, 9, 47, 49, 50, 53, 60, 62, 86, 95, 105, 106, 109, 111
Ruffo-Ciccolellas, 135
Ruhlman's Band, 77
Russo, Anthony R., 111
Russo, Domenick, 46
Russo, Domenico, 43, 126, 127
Russo, Frank, 46, 48, 52
Russo, Giovanni, 43, 46

Russo, Giuseppe, 41
Russo, John, 113, 43, 49, 61
Russo, Joseph, 154
Russo, Lucie, 116
Russo, M., 106
Russo, M.J., 106
Rutgers University, 102
Ruvo del Monte, 37
Ruzzi, Zepito, 24
Ryder, Nellie J., 9

Sabary, Victor, 103
Sacchetti, Prof., 31
Sacchitelli, Giuseppe, 47
Sacchitelli, Joseph, 59
Sacco and Vanzetti, 135
Sacco-Vanzetti Trial, 80
Sacred Heart, church of, 139
Saint Anne Society, 68
Saint Francis, church of, 23
Saint Gabriel Society, 68
Saint Joachim's A.C., 68
Saint Joseph Society, 68
Saint Lucy Filippini Society, 68
Saint Michael the Archangel Society, 37
Salamandra, Leo, 44, 46
Salamandra, Louis, 44
Salamandra, Luigi, 46
Salamandra, Maury, 122
Salamandra, Michael, 100
Salamandra, Rosato, 42
Salamandra, Tito, 52, 106
Salamandra, Umberto, 98
Salerno, Angelo, 45, 47, 86, 125, 126
Salvante, Rose, 114
Salvatore, Arthur A., 83, 94, 111, 112
Salvatore, Elizabeth, 105, 106
Salvatore, Giuseppe, 46, 105
Salvatore, Joseph John, 101
Salvatore, Joseph, 58
Salvatore, Josephine, 82, 106, 122
Salvatore, Reynold A., 101, 122
Samelli, 130
San Calogero Society, 68
San Calogero, feast of, 5, 27
San Donato, 26
San Donato, feast of, 25
San Fele, 19, 21, 37
San Filippo, Samuel, 115
San Filippon, Gaetano, 50
San Francesco Society, 37

INDEX

INDEX

INDEX